Pescatarian Air Fryer Cookbook for Beginners

1000 Days of Fresh, Tasty Pescatarian Recipes for Your Air Fryer to Kickstart The Healthy Lifestyle on A Budget

Susia Hall

Table of Contents

Introduction

The Pescatarian diet is one of the similar diet plans compare with the Mediterranean diet because both the diet are focused on vegetarian food and allows seafood to meet their protein requirements. The Pescatarian diet completely avoids meats, poultry, pork, and lamb because they contain saturated fat. Some of the Pescatarian diet followers allow eggs and dairy products into their products but some are not as it is their personal preference. The Pescatarian word is made an Italic world 'peace means 'fish, and vegetarian. Fish and seafood like crab, oyster, shrimp, and more are some of the primary sources of protein in the Pescatarian diet. It is recommended to consume 5 portions (each portion 80 gm) of vegetables and fruits daily. Also, recommend consuming at least two or more portion of fish and seafood in a week.

Vegetarian foods are rich in fibers, vitamins, minerals, and nutrients like magnesium, potassium, iron, and more. Fish and seafood make your diet protein-rich, it also contains omega-3 fatty acids which help to reduce oxidative stress and the risk of heart-related disease. The diet comes with various kinds of health benefits which are discussed late in chapter-1. This cookbook contains a healthy Pescatarian diet with a healthy cooking method popularly known as an air fryer. All the recipes written in this book are preparing using an air fryer oven.

This cookbook contains tasty, healthy and delicious Pescatarian diet recipes that come from different categories like breakfast, fish, seafood, vegetable, side dishes, snacks, appetizers. The recipes written in this book are unique and written into an easily understandable form. All the recipes are written with their preparation and cooking time followed by step-by-step cooking instructions. The recipes written in this book are ends with their nutritional value information. The nutritional value information will help to keep track of daily calorie consumption. The book also contains 30 days meal plan. There are various cookbooks are available in the market on this topic thanks for choosing my book. I hope you love and enjoy all the recipes written in this cookbook.

Chapter 1: The Basics of Pescatarian Diet

What is Pescatarian Diet?

A Pescatarian diet is one of the healthy eating habits followed by most people. The diet is similar to a vegetarian diet except the Pescatarian diet allows to eat fish and all kinds of seafood but eliminates animal products such as meats and poultry. The Pescatarian diet is mainly focused on eating vegetarian plant base food and seafood. Some people include dairy and eggs into their diet some are not as this is their personal preference. The Pescatarian diet allows you to consume protein from plant-based food such as nuts, legumes, whole grains, healthy fats with seafood plays a key role to provide enough protein to your body. Seafood such as fish, shrimp, crab, oyster, and more are the main source of animal protein.

The Pescatarian diet is somewhat similar to the Mediterranean diet because in both diets fish is one of the primary sources of protein. The diet contains nutrient-dense food which is high in fiber and low in calories. If your main goal is weight loss then the Pescatarian diet is one of the best diets that help to lose weight. The diet will give you long-term weight loss benefits. The seafood consumes during the diet is one of the best sources of omega-3 fatty acids which offers various kinds of health benefits.

Principles of Pescatarian Diet

The Pescatarian diet mainly depends on five major principles which are mention as follows.

1. **Seafood is the primary source of animal protein**

    Fish and other seafood like shrimp, crab, mussels, oyster, and more are a rich source of animal protein. It is recommended to eat at least two meals of fish and seafood each week to fulfil the body's protein needs. It is better and safe to eat fish and seafood meals several times a week.

2. **Consume lots of plant-based protein**

Consumption of plant base proteins into the diet is one of the inexpensive ways to meet your daily protein needs. The foods like lentils, beans, nuts, seeds, and soy products such as tofu and temph are protein reach foods. Most plant-based foods are high in fiber and rich in vitamins and minerals.

3. Add lots of vegetables and fruits

The Pescatarian diet increases the high intake of vegetables and fruits into your diet. Fruits and vegetables contain antioxidants, phytochemicals, essential vitamins, and minerals.

4. Concentrate on fiber-rich foods

Increase the intake of fiber-rich carbohydrate food will help to reduce the risk of diabetes, heart-related disease, and chronic disease. These foods include lentils, beans, fruits, vegetables, whole grains, sweet potatoes, potatoes, corn, and peas. These foods are rich in fiber, healthy fats, magnesium, iron, and vitamins.

5. Make sure healthy fats are included in the diet

Eat healthy fats during the Pescatarian diet from olive oil, nuts, avocado, and seeds with fish which are high in omega-3 fatty acids. These fish includes halibut, salmon, sardines, herrings, and more. The omega-3 fatty acids not only help to reduce the risk of a heart attack but also improve your heart health and keep you away from heart-related diseases.

Health Benefits of Pescatarian Diet

The Pescatarian diet is one of the best ways to consume healthy, delicious, and nutrient-rich food to improve your health. The diet comes with various types of health benefits, some of them are mention as follows:

- **Help to reduce the weight**

The Pescatarian diet allows eating low calorie, high in fiber, less saturated, natural, and healthy protein-rich food. It is one of the healthy ways to lose extra weight. The Pescatarian diet allows eating at least two meals of fish in a week. Fish are the primary source of animal proteins, the proteins help to burn the extra fats when it is paired with regular exercise.

- **Reduce the risk of Heart Disease**

The Pescatarian diet includes fish and seafood's so it is one of the best sources of Omega-3 fatty acids, fibers, antioxidants, and low in saturated fats. The omega-3 fatty acids have anti-inflammatory properties which help to lower the risk of heart-related diseases like sudden cardiac death, stroke, heart attack, and more. The diet not only reduces heart-related disease but also makes your heart strong and healthy.

- **Improves your brain health**

The near about 60 percent of our brains are fats. The omega-3 fatty acids play an important role to improve brain functions and also repair your damaged brain cells. It is also effective in the treatment of Alzheimer's disease. Omega-3 fatty acids are essential to improve your brain health and improve your mood and focus.

- **Reduce the risk of diabetes and inflammation**

The Pescatarian diet is a plant-based diet that allows fish and seafood to meet the daily protein needs. The plant-based diet helps to reduce the risk of type-2 diabetes and metabolic syndromes like obesity, high blood pressure, and insulin resistance. The presence of omega-3 fatty acids helps to reduce inflammation. The plant-based diet rich in antioxidants and has anti-inflammatory properties which help to reduce the risk of diabetes.

- **Low Mortality compares to non-vegetarian**

The Pescatarian diet is plant-based. Most of the studies conducted over plant base and non-vegetarian diet shows that the diet which is higher in plant-based foods are lower the risk of cardiovascular diseases compare with non-vegetarian meat-eaters.

- **Reduce the risk of cancer**

The Pescatarian diet helps to lower the overall cancer risk. Plant-based food such as vegetables, fruits, legumes, whole grains, and nuts are rich in fiber, essential vitamins, nutrients, and minerals. Most of the researches show that eating such nutrient-rich food helps to lower the rate of cancer. Plants food contains phytochemicals that protect our body cells from damage. Plant-based food is also rich in fibers which reduce the risk of breast cancer and colorectal cancer.

Foods Allowed During Pescatarian Diet

The Pescatarian diet is somewhat similar to the Mediterranean diet plan because in both the diet fish and seafood are allowed instead of meat and poultry to meet the need for protein. The following foods list that allowed during the Pescatarian diet is given as follows.

1. **Seafood**

Seafood such as fish, crab, oyster, shrimp, and more are used as the primary source of protein in the Pescatarian diet. The seafood is high in iodine, protein and also contains omega-3 fatty acids. The omega-3 fatty acid helps to reduce the risk of heart-related disease, stroke, and heart attack. Ii helps to improve brain functions and also effective to improve mental conditions like depression.

The Food allowed in this category includes.

Fish: Salmon, Tuna, Trout, Mackerel, Sardines, sea bass, and herring.

Shell Fish: Oyster, shrimp, crab, lobster, mussels, scallops, octopus, squid, and clams.

2. **Vegetables and fruits**

The Pescatarian diet is incomplete without vegetables and fruits. The vegetables and fruits are rich in fiber, vitamins, nutrients, and minerals. It helps to control blood sugar level, reduce the risk of heart disease, good for eye and also help to reduce the risk of some cancers. Some people recommend that to eat at least 5 portions of the vegetables and fruits each day. A single portion is 80 grams so you need a total of 400 grams daily.

The Food allowed in this category includes.

Vegetables: Broccoli, Bell Peppers, Cucumber, Garlic, Green beans, Onion, Spinach, Asparagus, Kale, Tomatoes, Potatoes, Carrots, Cauliflower, etc.

Fruits: Apple, Berries, Oranges, Pears, Grapes, Plums, Watermelon, Bananas, etc.

3. Legumes, lentils, nuts, and seeds

The legumes, lentils, nuts, and seeds are rich in protein, fiber, vitamins, minerals, and healthy fats. They are rich in antioxidants also help to reduce oxidative stress and also help to repair the body cells. These foods are low in calories, reduce inflammation and help to control blood sugar levels.

The Food allowed in this category includes.

Legume & Lentils: Bean, Peas, Soybean (Tofu), Chickpeas, etc.

Nuts and Seeds: Peanuts, Chia seeds, Flax seeds, Pumpkin seeds, Cashew, Hemp seeds, Pecans, Hazelnuts, Walnuts, etc.

4. Eggs and Dairy Products

The eggs and dairy products are optional, some peoples include them into diet and some are not. It depends on your personal preference. There are lots of options available in the dairy products proffered low-fat dairy products. Dairy products are one of the best sources of calcium, protein, phosphorus, and potassium. This is essential to improve your heart, bones, and muscles' health.

The Food allowed in this category includes.

Eggs (optional)

Dairy Products (Optional): Milk, Milk alternatives (Almond milk, Oat milk, Coconut milk, Cashew milk, Soy milk), Greek Yogurt, Low-fat cheese, etc.

5. Whole Grains

The whole grains are one of the best sources of fibers and nutrients like potassium, selenium, iron, B complex vitamins, folate, and magnesium. It helps to maintain your blood sugar level and lower cholesterol level and also effective to prevent some types of cancer.

The Food allowed in this category includes.

Whole Grains: Wheat flour, Whole cornmeal, Bulgur, Brown rice, and Oatmeal.

Food to Avoid

Non-vegetarian foods such as meats, poultry, beef, pork, lamb are strictly avoided in the Pescatarian diet because meat contains saturated fats which are also known as bad fats. The bad fats are associated with an increase in the risk of diabetes and heart-related diseases. Only vegetarian and seafood are allowed during the Pescatarian diet.

What is an Air Fryer?

The air fryer is one of the convection oven-type devices used to fry your food by using very few fats and oils. It takes 80 % fewer fats and oil to cook your food as compared with the traditional deep frying method. The air fryer is working on a hot air circulation mechanism. It blows hot air (400 °F) into the cooking chamber with the help of a convection fan. It makes your food crisp from the outside and tender from the inside without changing the taste and texture of the food like deep-fried food. If you love to eat fried food but are worried about extra calorie intake then an air fryer is one of the best healthy cooking options available in the market. The air fryer not only cooks your food faster but also gives you even cooking results every time you cook your food into an air fryer.

Chapter 2: Breakfast

Healthy Egg Bites

Preparation Time: 10 minutes
Cooking Time: 13 minutes
Serve: 4

Ingredients:

- 4 eggs, lightly beaten
- ¼ cup cheddar cheese, shredded
- ½ cup bell pepper, diced
- ½ cup almond milk
- ¼ tsp garlic powder
- Pepper
- Salt

Directions:

1. Preheat the air fryer to 325 F.
2. Add all ingredients into the bowl and whisk until well combined.
3. Spray silicone muffin molds with cooking spray.
4. Pour egg mixture into the silicone muffin mold and place it in the air fryer basket and cook for 8-10 minutes.
5. Serve and enjoy.

Nutritional Value (Amount per Serving):

- Calories 125
- Fat 8.1 g
- Carbohydrates 2.8 g
- Sugar 2.1 g
- Protein 9.8 g
- Cholesterol 178 mg

Easy Potato Wedges

Preparation Time: 10 minutes
Cooking Time: 10 minutes
Serve: 6

Ingredients:

- 2 lbs potatoes, cut into wedges
- 2 tbsp chipotle seasoning
- ¼ cup olive oil
- Pepper
- Salt

Directions:

1. Add potato wedges into the bowl.
2. Add remaining ingredients over potato wedges and toss well.
3. Transfer potato wedges into the air fryer basket and cook for 10 minutes. Turn potato wedges halfway through.
4. Serve and enjoy.

Nutritional Value (Amount per Serving):

- Calories 174
- Fat 8.6 g
- Carbohydrates 23.8 g
- Sugar 1.7 g
- Protein 2.5 g
- Cholesterol 0 mg

Sweet Potatoes & Brussels Sprouts

Preparation Time: 10 minutes
Cooking Time: 20 minutes
Serve: 4

Ingredients:

- 2 sweet potatoes, wash, and cut into 1-inch pieces
- 1 lb Brussels sprouts, cut in half
- ¼ tsp chili powder
- 2 tbsp olive oil
- ¼ tsp garlic powder
- ½ tsp pepper
- 1 tsp salt

Directions:

1. Preheat the air fryer to 400 F.
2. Add sweet potatoes, Brussels sprouts, and remaining ingredients into the bowl and toss until well coated.
3. Transfer sweet potatoes and Brussels sprouts mixture into the air fryer basket and cook for 20 minutes. Stir halfway through.
4. Serve and enjoy.

Nutritional Value (Amount per Serving):

- Calories 135
- Fat 7.4 g
- Carbohydrates 17.2 g
- Sugar 3.9 g
- Protein 4.4 g
- Cholesterol 0 mg

Healthy Spinach Frittata

Preparation Time: 10 minutes
Cooking Time: 8 minutes
Serve: 1

Ingredients:

- 2 eggs, lightly beaten
- ¼ cup spinach, chopped
- ¼ cup tomatoes, chopped
- 2 tbsp almond milk
- ¼ tsp garlic powder
- 1 tbsp parmesan cheese, grated
- Pepper
- Salt

Directions:

1. In a bowl, whisk eggs. Add remaining ingredients and whisk until well combined.
2. Spray small air fryer pan with cooking spray.
3. Pour egg mixture into the prepared pan.
4. Place pan into the air fryer basket and cook at 330 F for 8 minutes.
5. Serve and enjoy.

Nutritional Value (Amount per Serving):

- Calories 190
- Fat 11.7 g
- Carbohydrates 4.3 g
- Sugar 3.3 g
- Protein 15.7 g
- Cholesterol 337 mg

Breakfast Potatoes

Preparation Time: 10 minutes
Cooking Time: 20 minutes
Serve: 6

Ingredients:

- 1 ½ lbs potatoes, diced into ½-inch cubes
- ¼ tsp chili powder
- ¼ tsp pepper
- 1 tsp paprika
- 1 tsp garlic powder
- 1 tbsp olive oil
- Salt

Directions:

1. Add potatoes and remaining ingredients into the bowl and toss well.
2. Add potatoes into the air fryer basket and cook at 400 F for 20 minutes. Stir potatoes halfway through.
3. Serve and enjoy.

Nutritional Value (Amount per Serving):

- Calories 105
- Fat 2.5 g
- Carbohydrates 18.5 g
- Sugar 1.5 g
- Protein 2.1 g
- Cholesterol 0 mg

Spinach Pepper Egg Bites

Preparation Time: 10 minutes
Cooking Time: 20 minutes
Serve: 6

Ingredients:

- 4 eggs
- 1/2 cup spinach, chopped
- 1/2 cup roasted peppers, chopped
- 1/8 cup almond milk
- 2 tbsp green onion, chopped
- 1/4 tsp salt

Directions:

1. Preheat the air fryer to 325 F.
2. In a bowl, whisk eggs with milk and salt. Add spinach, green onion, and peppers and stir to combine.
3. Pour egg mixture into the silicone muffin molds.
4. Place muffin molds into the air fryer basket and cook for 12-15 minutes.
5. Serve and enjoy.

Nutritional Value (Amount per Serving):

- Calories 60
- Fat 4.2 g
- Carbohydrates 1.7 g
- Sugar 1.1 g
- Protein 4.1 g
- Cholesterol 109 mg

Egg Cheese Muffins

Preparation Time: 10 minutes
Cooking Time: 20 minutes
Serve: 6

Ingredients:

- 4 eggs
- 1 scoop whey protein powder
- 2 tbsp butter, melted
- 4 oz cream cheese
- Pepper
- Salt

Directions:

1. Preheat the air fryer to 325 F.
2. Add all ingredients into the bowl and whisk until combine.
3. Pour batter into the silicone muffin molds.
4. Place muffin molds into the air fryer basket and cook for 20 minutes.
5. Serve and enjoy.

Nutritional Value (Amount per Serving):

- Calories 165
- Fat 13.7 g
- Carbohydrates 1.4 g
- Sugar 0.4 g
- Protein 8.9 g
- Cholesterol 151 mg

Mushroom Spinach Muffins

Preparation Time: 10 minutes
Cooking Time: 15 minutes
Serve: 6

Ingredients:

- 5 eggs
- 1 cup spinach, chopped
- 1/4 tsp onion powder
- 1/2 cup mushrooms, chopped
- 1/4 tsp garlic powder
- Pepper
- Salt

Directions:

1. Preheat the air fryer to 375 F.
2. In a bowl, whisk eggs with garlic powder, onion powder, pepper, and salt. Add spinach and mushrooms and stir well.
3. Pour egg mixture into the 6 silicone muffin molds.
4. Place muffin molds into the air fryer basket and cook for 10-12 minutes.
5. Serve and enjoy.

Nutritional Value (Amount per Serving):

- Calories 75
- Fat 5 g
- Carbohydrates 0.9 g
- Sugar 0.5 g
- Protein 6.1 g
- Cholesterol 140 mg

Egg Veggie Soufflé

Preparation Time: 10 minutes

Cooking Time: 20 minutes

Serve: 4

Ingredients:

- 4 eggs
- 1/2 cup mushrooms, chopped
- 1 tsp onion powder
- 1 tsp garlic powder
- 1/2 cup broccoli florets, chopped
- Pepper
- Salt

Directions:

1. Preheat the air fryer to 350 F.
2. Spray four ramekins with cooking spray and set aside.
3. In a bowl, whisk eggs with onion powder, garlic powder, pepper, and salt. Add mushrooms and broccoli and stir well.
4. Pour egg mixture into the prepared ramekins.
5. Place ramekins into the air fryer basket and cook for 20 minutes.
6. Serve and enjoy.

Nutritional Value (Amount per Serving):

- Calories 85
- Fat 5.1 g
- Carbohydrates 2.4 g
- Sugar 1.1 g
- Protein 7.1 g
- Cholesterol 186 mg

Italian Egg Muffins

Preparation Time: 10 minutes
Cooking Time: 20 minutes
Serve: 12

Ingredients:

- 6 eggs
- 3 cherry tomatoes, chopped
- 4 sun-dried tomatoes, chopped
- 1/2 cup feta cheese, crumbled
- 2 tsp olive oil
- Pepper
- Salt

Directions:

1. Preheat the air fryer to 350 F.
2. In a bowl, whisk eggs with pepper and salt. Add remaining ingredients and stir well.
3. Pour egg mixture into the 12 silicone muffin molds.
4. Place half muffin molds into the air fryer basket and cook for 12-15 minutes.
5. Serve and enjoy.

Nutritional Value (Amount per Serving):

- Calories 65
- Fat 4.4 g
- Carbohydrates 2.1 g
- Sugar 1.2 g
- Protein 4 g
- Cholesterol 87 mg

Chapter 3: Fish & Seafood

Marinated Ginger Garlic Salmon

Preparation Time: 10 minutes
Cooking Time: 10 minutes
Serve: 2

Ingredients:

- 2 salmon fillets, skinless & boneless
- 1 1/2 tbsp mirin
- 1 1/2 tbsp soy sauce
- 1 tbsp olive oil
- 2 tbsp green onion, minced
- 1 tbsp ginger, grated
- 1 tsp garlic, minced

Directions:

1. Add mirin, soy sauce, oil, green onion, ginger, and garlic into the zip-lock bag and mix well.
2. Add fish fillets into the bag, seal the bag, and place in the refrigerator for 30 minutes.
3. Preheat the air fryer to 360 F.
4. Spray air fryer basket with cooking spray.
5. Place marinated salmon fillets into the air fryer basket and cook for 10 minutes.
6. Serve and enjoy.

Nutritional Value (Amount per Serving):

- Calories 334
- Fat 18.2 g
- Carbohydrates 9 g
- Sugar 3.4 g
- Protein 35.7 g
- Cholesterol 78 mg

Chili Honey Salmon

Preparation Time: 10 minutes
Cooking Time: 12 minutes
Serve: 2

Ingredients:

- 2 salmon fillets
- 3 tbsp honey
- 1/2 tbsp chili flakes
- 1/2 tsp chili powder
- 1/2 tsp turmeric
- 1 tsp ground coriander
- 1/8 tsp pepper
- 1/8 tsp salt

Directions:

1. Add honey to microwave-safe bowl and heat for 10 seconds.
2. Add chili flakes, chili powder, turmeric, coriander, pepper, and salt into the honey and mix well.
3. Brush salmon fillets with honey mixture.
4. Place salmon fillets into the air fryer basket and cook at 400 F for 12 minutes.
5. Serve and enjoy.

Nutritional Value (Amount per Serving):

- Calories 336
- Fat 11.2 g
- Carbohydrates 26.8 g
- Sugar 26 g
- Protein 34.8 g
- Cholesterol 78 mg

Tender & Juicy Honey Glazed Salmon

Preparation Time: 10 minutes
Cooking Time: 10 minutes
Serve: 4

Ingredients:

- 4 salmon fillets
- 1 tbsp honey
- 1/2 tsp red chili flakes, crushed
- 1 tsp sesame seeds, toasted
- 1 1/2 tsp olive oil
- 1 tbsp coconut aminos
- Pepper
- Salt

Directions:

1. Place salmon fillets into the bowl. In a small bowl, mix coconut aminos, oil, pepper, and salt and pour over fish fillets. Mix well.
2. Cover bowl and place in the refrigerator for 20 minutes.
3. Preheat the air fryer to 400 F.
4. Place marinated salmon fillets into the air fryer basket and cook for 8 minutes.
5. Brush fish fillets with honey and sprinkle with chili flakes and sesame seeds and cook for 2 minutes more.
6. Serve and enjoy.

Nutritional Value (Amount per Serving):

- Calories 271
- Fat 13.1 g
- Carbohydrates 4.5 g
- Sugar 4.3 g
- Protein 34.7 g
- Cholesterol 78 mg

Easy Herbed Salmon

Preparation Time: 10 minutes
Cooking Time: 5 minutes
Serve: 2

Ingredients:

- 2 salmon fillets
- 1 tbsp butter
- 2 tbsp olive oil
- 1/4 tsp paprika
- 1 tsp herb de Provence
- Pepper
- Salt

Directions:

1. Brush salmon fillets with oil and sprinkle with paprika, herb de Provence, pepper, and salt.
2. Place salmon fillets into the air fryer basket and cook at 390 F for 5 minutes.
3. Melt butter in a pan and pour over cooked salmon fillets.
4. Serve and enjoy.

Nutritional Value (Amount per Serving):

- Calories 407
- Fat 30.8 g
- Carbohydrates 0.2 g
- Sugar 0 g
- Protein 34.6 g
- Cholesterol 94 mg

Lemon Butter Salmon

Preparation Time: 10 minutes
Cooking Time: 12 minutes
Serve: 2

Ingredients:

- 2 salmon fillets
- 1/2 tsp soy sauce
- 3/4 tsp dill, chopped
- 1 tsp garlic, minced
- 1 1/2 tbsp fresh lemon juice
- 2 tbsp butter, melted
- Pepper
- Salt

Directions:

1. Preheat the air fryer to 400 F.
2. In a small bowl, mix butter, lemon juice, garlic, dill, soy sauce, pepper, and salt.
3. Brush salmon fillets with butter mixture and place into the air fryer basket and cook for 10-12 minutes.
4. Pour the remaining butter mixture over cooked salmon fillets and serve.

Nutritional Value (Amount per Serving):

- Calories 344
- Fat 22.6 g
- Carbohydrates 1.1 g
- Sugar 0.3 g
- Protein 35 g
- Cholesterol 109 mg

Perfect Parmesan Salmon

Preparation Time: 10 minutes
Cooking Time: 10 minutes
Serve: 4

Ingredients:

- 4 salmon fillets
- 1/4 cup parmesan cheese, shredded
- 1/4 tsp dried dill
- 1/2 tbsp Dijon mustard
- 4 tbsp mayonnaise
- 1 lemon juice
- Pepper
- Salt

Directions:

1. In a small bowl, mix cheese, dill, mustard, mayonnaise, lemon juice, pepper, and salt.
2. Place salmon fillets into the air fryer basket and brush with cheese mixture.
3. Cook salmon fillets at 400 F for 10 minutes.
4. Serve and enjoy.

Nutritional Value (Amount per Serving):

- Calories 294
- Fat 16 g
- Carbohydrates 3.7 g
- Sugar 1 g
- Protein 34.8 g
- Cholesterol 82 mg

Quick & Easy Salmon

Preparation Time: 10 minutes
Cooking Time: 8 minutes
Serve: 4

Ingredients:

- 4 salmon fillets
- 1/2 tsp smoked paprika
- 1 tsp garlic powder
- 1 tbsp olive oil
- Pepper
- Salt

Directions:

1. Preheat the air fryer to 400 F.
2. Brush salmon fillets with oil and sprinkle with smoked paprika, garlic powder, pepper, and salt.
3. Place salmon fillets into the air fryer basket and cook for 8 minutes.
4. Serve and enjoy.

Nutritional Value (Amount per Serving):

- Calories 269
- Fat 14.5 g
- Carbohydrates 0.7 g
- Sugar 0.2 g
- Protein 34.7 g
- Cholesterol 78 mg

Healthy Salmon Patties

Preparation Time: 10 minutes
Cooking Time: 8 minutes
Serve: 6

Ingredients:

- 1 egg
- 1 tsp paprika
- 2 green onions, minced
- 2 tbsp fresh coriander, chopped
- 14 oz can salmon, drain & mince
- Pepper
- Salt

Directions:

1. Preheat the air fryer to 360 F.
2. Add all ingredients into the bowl and mix until well combined.
3. Spray air fryer basket with cooking spray.
4. Make the equal shape of patties from the mixture and place into the air fryer basket and cook for 8 minutes.
5. Serve and enjoy.

Nutritional Value (Amount per Serving):

- Calories 105
- Fat 4.8 g
- Carbohydrates 0.7 g
- Sugar 0.2 g
- Protein 14.2 g
- Cholesterol 64 mg

Flavorful Salmon Fillets

Preparation Time: 10 minutes
Cooking Time: 10 minutes
Serve: 2

Ingredients:

- 2 salmon fillets, boneless
- 1/2 tsp garlic powder
- 1/2 tsp ground cumin
- 1/2 tsp chili powder
- 2 tbsp fresh lemon juice
- 2 tbsp olive oil
- Pepper
- Salt

Directions:

1. In a small bowl, mix oil, lemon juice, chili powder, ground cumin, garlic powder, pepper, and salt.
2. Brush salmon fillets with oil mixture and place into the air fryer basket and cook at 400 F for 10 minutes.
3. Serve and enjoy.

Nutritional Value (Amount per Serving):

- Calories 366
- Fat 25.4 g
- Carbohydrates 1.5 g
- Sugar 0.6 g
- Protein 35 g
- Cholesterol 78 mg

Basil Cheese Salmon

Preparation Time: 10 minutes
Cooking Time: 7 minutes
Serve: 4

Ingredients:

- 4 salmon fillets
- 1/4 cup parmesan cheese, grated
- 5 fresh basil leaves, minced
- 2 tbsp mayonnaise
- 1/2 lemon juice
- Pepper
- Salt

Directions:

1. Preheat the air fryer to 400 F.
2. Brush salmon fillets with lemon juice and season with pepper and salt.
3. In a small bowl, mix mayonnaise, basil, and cheese.
4. Spray air fryer basket with cooking spray.
5. Place salmon fillets into the air fryer basket and brush with mayonnaise mixture and cook for 7 minutes.
6. Serve and enjoy.

Nutritional Value (Amount per Serving):

- Calories 414
- Fat 22.4 g
- Carbohydrates 1.8 g
- Sugar 0.5 g
- Protein 46.6 g
- Cholesterol 110 mg

Sriracha Salmon

Preparation Time: 10 minutes
Cooking Time: 12 minutes
Serve: 4

Ingredients:

- 1 lb salmon fillets
- 1 tbsp soy sauce
- 1/2 cup honey
- 4 tbsp sriracha

Directions:

1. In a bowl, mix soy sauce, honey, and sriracha. Add fish fillets and mix well, cover and place in the refrigerator for 30 minutes.
2. Spray air fryer basket with cooking spray.
3. Place marinated salmon fillets into the air fryer basket and cook at 400 F for 12 minutes.
4. Serve and enjoy.

Nutritional Value (Amount per Serving):

- Calories 296
- Fat 7 g
- Carbohydrates 38.2 g
- Sugar 34.9 g
- Protein 22.4 g
- Cholesterol 50 mg

Garlic Brown Sugar Salmon

Preparation Time: 10 minutes

Cooking Time: 10 minutes

Serve: 4

Ingredients:

- 1 lb salmon fillets
- 3/4 tsp garlic powder
- 1 tsp Italian seasoning
- 1/2 tsp smoked paprika
- 3/4 tsp chili powder
- 2 tbsp brown sugar
- Pepper
- Salt

Directions:

1. In a small bowl, mix garlic powder, Italian seasoning, paprika, chili powder, brown sugar, pepper, and salt and rub over salmon fillets.
2. Spray air fryer basket with cooking spray.
3. Place salmon fillets into the air fryer basket and cook at 400 F for 10 minutes.
4. Serve and enjoy.

Nutritional Value (Amount per Serving):

- Calories 175
- Fat 7.5 g
- Carbohydrates 5.4 g
- Sugar 4.7 g
- Protein 22.2 g
- Cholesterol 51 mg

Blackened Salmon

Preparation Time: 10 minutes
Cooking Time: 7 minutes
Serve: 4

Ingredients:

- 4 salmon fillets
- 3/4 tsp dried thyme
- 3/4 tsp dried oregano
- 1/2 tsp garlic powder
- 1/2 tsp cayenne
- 1 tbsp sweet paprika
- 1 tbsp olive oil
- Pepper
- Salt

Directions:

1. Preheat the air fryer to 400 F.
2. In a small bowl, mix thyme, oregano, garlic powder, cayenne, paprika, pepper, and salt.
3. Brush salmon fillets with oil and coat with spice and herb mixture.
4. Place salmon fillets into the air fryer basket and cook for 7 minutes.
5. Serve and enjoy.

Nutritional Value (Amount per Serving):

- Calories 274
- Fat 14.8 g
- Carbohydrates 1.7 g
- Sugar 0.3 g
- Protein 34.9 g
- Cholesterol 78 mg

Honey Mustard Salmon

Preparation Time: 10 minutes
Cooking Time: 10 minutes
Serve: 2

Ingredients:

- 2 salmon fillets
- 1 tsp paprika
- 1 tsp olive oil
- 1 tbsp Dijon mustard
- 1 tbsp honey
- Pepper
- Salt

Directions:

1. Preheat the air fryer to 400 F.
2. In a small bowl, mix honey, mustard, oil, paprika, pepper, and salt.
3. Brush salmon fillets with honey mixture and place into the air fryer basket and cook for 10 minutes.
4. Serve and enjoy.

Nutritional Value (Amount per Serving):

- Calories 296
- Fat 13.8 g
- Carbohydrates 9.7 g
- Sugar 8.8 g
- Protein 35.1 g
- Cholesterol 78 mg

Chili Sauce Salmon

Preparation Time: 10 minutes
Cooking Time: 15 minutes
Serve: 2

Ingredients:

- 1 lb salmon fillets
- 1 1/2 tbsp sriracha
- 1/3 cup Thai chili sauce
- 1/2 cup mayonnaise
- Pepper
- Salt

Directions:

1. In a small bowl, mix sriracha, chili sauce, mayonnaise, pepper, and salt.
2. Brush salmon fillets with sriracha mixture and place into the air fryer basket and cook at 400 F for 13-15 minutes.
3. Serve and enjoy.

Nutritional Value (Amount per Serving):

- Calories 541
- Fat 33.6 g
- Carbohydrates 16.3 g
- Sugar 3.8 g
- Protein 44.5 g
- Cholesterol 115 mg

Easy Cod Fillet

Preparation Time: 10 minutes
Cooking Time: 10 minutes
Serve: 1

Ingredients:

- 3 oz cod fillet
- 1/8 tsp garlic powder
- 1 lemon slice
- Pepper
- Salt

Directions:

1. Season cod fillet with garlic powder, pepper, and salt.
2. Place cod fillet into the air fryer basket and top with a lemon slice.
3. Cook cod fillet at 375 F for 10 minutes.
4. Serve and enjoy.

Nutritional Value (Amount per Serving):

- Calories 72
- Fat 0.4 g
- Carbohydrates 1 g
- Sugar 0.3 g
- Protein 16.9 g
- Cholesterol 27 mg

Lemon Dill Cod

Preparation Time: 10 minutes
Cooking Time: 10 minutes
Serve: 4

Ingredients:

- 4 cod fillets
- 1 tsp dried dill
- 2 tbsp lemon juice
- 1 1/2 tbsp garlic, minced
- 1/4 cup butter, melted
- Pepper
- Salt

Directions:

1. Preheat the air fryer to 370 F.
2. In a bowl, mix butter, garlic, lemon juice, dill, pepper, and salt. Add cod fillets and coat well.
3. Place fish fillets into the air fryer basket and cook for 10 minutes.
4. Serve and enjoy.

Nutritional Value (Amount per Serving):

- Calories 204
- Fat 12.3 g
- Carbohydrates 1.4 g
- Sugar 0.2 g
- Protein 21.2 g
- Cholesterol 73 mg

Quick Chili Lime Cod

Preparation Time: 10 minutes
Cooking Time: 10 minutes
Serve: 2

Ingredients:

- 2 cod fillets
- 1 tbsp olive oil
- 1/4 tsp ground cumin
- 1/2 tsp garlic powder
- 1/2 tsp chili powder
- 1/2 tsp dried oregano
- 1 tsp dried parsley
- 3/4 tsp smoked paprika
- 1 lime zest, grated
- Salt

Directions:

1. Add oil, cumin, garlic powder, chili powder, oregano, parsley, paprika, and salt into the zip-lock bag and mix well.
2. Add cod fillets into the zip-lock bag, seal bag, and place in the refrigerator for 30 minutes.
3. Preheat the air fryer to 380 F.
4. Place marinated fish fillets into the air fryer basket and cook for 10 minutes.
5. Serve and enjoy.

Nutritional Value (Amount per Serving):

- Calories 159
- Fat 8.3 g
- Carbohydrates 1.7 g
- Sugar 0.3 g
- Protein 20.4 g
- Cholesterol 40 mg

Parmesan Cod Fillets

Preparation Time: 10 minutes
Cooking Time: 7 minutes
Serve: 2

Ingredients:

- 2 cod fillets
- 1/4 cup parmesan cheese, grated
- 1/2 cup whole-wheat breadcrumbs
- 1/4 tsp Italian seasoning
- 2 tbsp olive oil
- Pepper
- Salt

Directions:

1. In a shallow dish, mix parmesan cheese, breadcrumbs, Italian seasoning, pepper, and salt.
2. Brush fish fillets with oil and coat with cheese mixture.
3. Place fish fillets into the air fryer basket and cook at 390 F for 7 minutes.
4. Serve and enjoy.

Nutritional Value (Amount per Serving):

- Calories 619
- Fat 34.6 g
- Carbohydrates 19.5 g
- Sugar 1.7 g
- Protein 47.6 g
- Cholesterol 115 mg

Miso Sea Bass Fillets

Preparation Time: 10 minutes
Cooking Time: 20 minutes
Serve: 2

Ingredients:

- 2 sea bass fillets
- 1/2 tsp ginger garlic paste
- 2 tbsp mirin
- 4 tbsp honey
- 1 tbsp vinegar
- 4 tbsp miso paste
- 1 tbsp olive oil
- Pepper
- Salt

Directions:

1. Preheat the air fryer to 375 F.
2. Spray fish fillets with cooking spray and season with pepper and salt.
3. Place fish fillets into the air fryer basket and cook for 15 minutes.
4. Meanwhile, heat oil in a pan over medium heat. Add miso paste, vinegar, honey, mirin, and ginger garlic paste and stir to combine.
5. Remove pan from heat. Brush fish fillets with a miso glaze.
6. Serve and enjoy.

Nutritional Value (Amount per Serving):

- Calories 408
- Fat 11.7 g
- Carbohydrates 50.8 g
- Sugar 40.7 g
- Protein 28 g
- Cholesterol 54 mg

Curried Cod Fillets

Preparation Time: 10 minutes
Cooking Time: 10 minutes
Serve: 2

Ingredients:

- 2 cod fillets
- 1/8 tsp smoked paprika
- 1/8 tsp curry powder
- 1/8 tsp garlic powder
- 1/2 tsp sugar
- 1/4 cup Italian dressing
- Pepper
- Salt

Directions:

1. Add fish fillets and remaining ingredients into the bowl and mix well. Cover and place in the refrigerator for 15 minutes.
2. Preheat the air fryer to 370 F.
3. Spray air fryer basket with cooking spray.
4. Place fish fillets into the air fryer basket and cook for 10 minutes.
5. Serve and enjoy.

Nutritional Value (Amount per Serving):

- Calories 181
- Fat 9.4 g
- Carbohydrates 4.4 g
- Sugar 3.5 g
- Protein 20.2 g
- Cholesterol 60 mg

Garlic Lemon Tilapia

Preparation Time: 10 minutes
Cooking Time: 10 minutes
Serve: 2

Ingredients:

- 2 tilapia fillets
- 1/2 tsp lemon pepper seasoning
- 1/2 tsp garlic powder
- Pepper
- Salt

Directions:

1. Preheat the air fryer to 360 F.
2. Spray fish fillets with cooking spray.
3. Season fish fillets with lemon pepper seasoning, garlic powder, pepper, and salt.
4. Place fish fillets into the air fryer basket and cook for 10 minutes.
5. Serve and enjoy.

Nutritional Value (Amount per Serving):

- Calories 97
- Fat 1.1 g
- Carbohydrates 0.9 g
- Sugar 0.2 g
- Protein 21.2 g
- Cholesterol 55 mg

Super Healthy Tilapia

Preparation Time: 10 minutes
Cooking Time: 10 minutes
Serve: 2

Ingredients:

- 2 tilapia fillets
- 1/4 tsp smoked paprika
- 1/2 tsp garlic powder
- 2 tsp olive oil
- Pepper
- Salt

Directions:

1. Preheat the air fryer to 390 F.
2. Brush fish fillets with oil and sprinkle with paprika, garlic powder, pepper, and salt.
3. Place fish fillets into the air fryer basket and cook for 10 minutes.
4. Serve and enjoy.

Nutritional Value (Amount per Serving):

- Calories 183
- Fat 6.7 g
- Carbohydrates 0.7 g
- Sugar 0.2 g
- Protein 32.2 g
- Cholesterol 85 mg

Flavorful Halibut

Preparation Time: 10 minutes
Cooking Time: 12 minutes
Serve: 2

Ingredients:

- 2 halibut fillets
- 1/2 tsp onion powder
- 1/2 tsp garlic powder
- 1/4 tsp chili powder
- Pepper
- Salt

Directions:

1. Spray fish fillets with cooking spray.
2. Season fish fillets with onion powder, garlic powder, chili powder, pepper, and salt.
3. Place fish fillets into the air fryer basket and cook for 12 minutes.
4. Serve and enjoy.

Nutritional Value (Amount per Serving):

- Calories 324
- Fat 6.8 g
- Carbohydrates 1.2 g
- Sugar 0.4 g
- Protein 60.7 g
- Cholesterol 93 mg

Crispy Crusted Halibut

Preparation Time: 10 minutes
Cooking Time: 10 minutes
Serve: 4

Ingredients:

- 4 halibut fillets
- 1/2 cup white wine
- 1/2 cup cornstarch
- 2 egg whites
- 1/2 cup whole-wheat breadcrumbs
- 1/2 cup pecan, crushed
- 1/2 tsp Italian seasoning
- Pepper
- Salt

Directions:

1. In a bowl, whisk together egg whites, cornstarch, and wine.
2. In a shallow dish, mix breadcrumbs, pecans, Italian seasoning, pepper, and salt.
3. Dredge the fish fillets into the egg mixture then coat with breadcrumb mixture.
4. Preheat the air fryer to 375 F.
5. Spray air fryer basket with cooking spray.
6. Place fish fillets into the air fryer basket and cook for 10 minutes.
7. Serve and enjoy.

Nutritional Value (Amount per Serving):

- Calories 467
- Fat 7.6 g
- Carbohydrates 25.3 g
- Sugar 1.2 g
- Protein 64.2 g
- Cholesterol 93 mg

Parmesan Halibut

Preparation Time: 10 minutes
Cooking Time: 15 minutes
Serve: 2

Ingredients:

- 2 halibut fillets
- 1/4 tsp garlic powder
- 1 tbsp parsley, chopped
- 1/4 cup parmesan cheese, grated
- 1/2 cup whole-wheat breadcrumbs
- 1/2 lemon juice
- 1 tbsp olive oil
- Pepper
- Salt

Directions:

1. In a shallow dish, mix breadcrumbs, cheese, parsley, garlic powder, pepper, and salt.
2. In a small bowl, mix oil and lemon juice.
3. Brush fish fillets with oil mixture and coat with breadcrumb mixture.
4. Place fish fillets into the air fryer basket and cook at 400 F for 12-15 minutes.
5. Serve and enjoy.

Nutritional Value (Amount per Serving):

- Calories 380
- Fat 13.7 g
- Carbohydrates 0.4 g
- Sugar 0.1 g
- Protein 60.6 g
- Cholesterol 93 mg

Garlic Herb Tilapia

Preparation Time: 10 minutes
Cooking Time: 12 minutes
Serve: 4

Ingredients:

- 4 tilapia fillets
- 1 tbsp olive oil
- 1 tbsp garlic herb seasoning

Directions:

1. Preheat the air fryer to 400 F.
2. Brush fish fillets with oil and sprinkle with seasoning.
3. Place fish fillets into the air fryer basket and cook for 12 minutes.
4. Serve and enjoy.

Nutritional Value (Amount per Serving):

- Calories 130
- Fat 4.5 g
- Carbohydrates 0 g
- Sugar 0 g
- Protein 22 g
- Cholesterol 100 mg

Crispy Catfish Fillets

Preparation Time: 10 minutes
Cooking Time: 20 minutes
Serve: 4

Ingredients:

- 4 catfish fillets
- 3 tsp Cajun seasoning
- 1 cup cornmeal
- Pepper
- Salt

Directions:

1. In a shallow dish, mix cornmeal, pepper, Cajun seasoning, and salt.
2. Coat fish fillets with cornmeal mixture and place into the air fryer basket and cook at 390 F for 15 minutes.
3. Turn temperature to 400 F and cook fish fillets for 5 minutes more.
4. Serve and enjoy.

Nutritional Value (Amount per Serving):

- Calories 326
- Fat 13.2 g
- Carbohydrates 23.5 g
- Sugar 0.2 g
- Protein 27.4 g
- Cholesterol 75 mg

Simple & Tasty Tilapia

Preparation Time: 10 minutes
Cooking Time: 5 minutes
Serve: 4

Ingredients:

- 1 egg, lightly beaten
- 1 tbsp old bay seasoning
- 1 cup whole-wheat breadcrumbs
- 4 tilapia fish fillets

Directions:

1. Preheat the air fryer to 400 F.
2. In a small dish, add egg and whisk well.
3. In a shallow dish, mix breadcrumbs and seasoning.
4. Dip fish fillets in egg then coat with breadcrumb mixture.
5. Place fish fillets into the air fryer basket and cook for 5 minutes.
6. Serve and enjoy.

Nutritional Value (Amount per Serving):

- Calories 266
- Fat 13.1 g
- Carbohydrates 23.1 g
- Sugar 1.1 g
- Protein 13.4 g
- Cholesterol 66 mg

Juicy & Tender Tilapia

Preparation Time: 10 minutes
Cooking Time: 10 minutes
Serve: 2

Ingredients:

- 2 tilapia fillets
- 1 tsp garlic, minced
- 2 tsp parsley, chopped
- 2 tsp chives, chopped
- 2 tsp olive oil
- Pepper
- Salt

Directions:

1. Preheat the air fryer to 400 F.
2. In a small bowl, mix oil, chives, parsley, garlic, pepper, and salt.
3. Brush fish fillets with oil mixture and place into the air fryer basket and cook for 10 minutes.
4. Serve and enjoy.

Nutritional Value (Amount per Serving):

- Calories 143
- Fat 5.7 g
- Carbohydrates 0.6 g
- Sugar 0 g
- Protein 22.2 g
- Cholesterol 100 mg

Simple Mahi Mahi

Preparation Time: 10 minutes
Cooking Time: 12 minutes
Serve: 4

Ingredients:

- 4 mahi-mahi fillets
- 2/3 cup butter
- Pepper
- Salt

Directions:

1. Preheat the air fryer to 350 F.
2. Season Mahi-mahi fillets with pepper and salt.
3. Place fish fillets into the air fryer basket and cook for 12 minutes.
4. Add butter into the pan and melt over medium heat.
5. Pour melted butter over fish fillets and serve.

Nutritional Value (Amount per Serving):

- Calories 361
- Fat 30.7 g
- Carbohydrates 0 g
- Sugar 0 g
- Protein 21.3 g
- Cholesterol 121 mg

Pesto Mahi Mahi

Preparation Time: 10 minutes
Cooking Time: 15 minutes
Serve: 2

Ingredients:

- 2 mahi-mahi fillets
- 3/4 cup basil pesto
- Pepper
- Salt

Directions:

1. Preheat the air fryer to 300 F.
2. Season fish fillets with pepper and salt.
3. Place fish fillets into the air fryer basket. Top fish with basil pesto and cook for 12-15 minutes.
4. Serve and enjoy.

Nutritional Value (Amount per Serving):

- Calories 92
- Fat 0.1 g
- Carbohydrates 0.3 g
- Sugar 0 g
- Protein 21.3 g
- Cholesterol 40 mg

Easy Lemon Dill Fish Fillets

Preparation Time: 10 minutes
Cooking Time: 14 minutes
Serve: 2

Ingredients:

- 2 mahi-mahi fillets
- 1 tbsp dill, chopped
- 2 lemon sliced
- 1 tbsp olive oil
- 1 tbsp lemon juice
- Pepper
- Salt

Directions:

1. In a small bowl, mix olive oil and lemon juice.
2. Season fish fillets with pepper and salt and brush with oil mixture.
3. Place fish fillets into the air fryer basket and top with dill and lemon slices and cook at 400 F for 12-14 minutes.
4. Serve and enjoy.

Nutritional Value (Amount per Serving):

- Calories 156
- Fat 7.1 g
- Carbohydrates 1.1 g
- Sugar 0.2 g
- Protein 21.4 g
- Cholesterol 40 mg

Delicious Tuna Patties

Preparation Time: 10 minutes
Cooking Time: 10 minutes
Serve: 5

Ingredients:

- 2 eggs, lightly beaten
- 15 oz can tuna, drained
- 1/2 tsp dried herbs
- 1/2 tsp garlic powder
- 2 tbsp onion, minced
- 1 celery stalk, chopped
- 3 tbsp parmesan cheese, grated
- 1/2 cup whole-wheat breadcrumbs
- 1 tbsp lemon juice
- 1 lemon zest
- Pepper
- Salt

Directions:

1. Add all ingredients into the bowl and mix until well combined.
2. Make equal shape of patties from mixture and place onto the parchment-lined baking sheet. Place patties in the refrigerator for 1 hour.
3. Spray air fryer basket with cooking spray.
4. Place patties into the air fryer basket and cook at 360 F for 10 minutes. Flip patties halfway through.
5. Serve and enjoy.

Nutritional Value (Amount per Serving):

- Calories 128
- Fat 2.5 g
- Carbohydrates 0.9 g
- Sugar 0.5 g
- Protein 24.1 g
- Cholesterol 91 mg

Cheesy Tuna Patties

Preparation Time: 10 minutes
Cooking Time: 10 minutes
Serve: 4

Ingredients:

- 1 egg
- 5.2 oz tuna, drained
- 1/2 tsp onion powder
- 1/2 tsp garlic powder
- 1 tsp paprika
- 2 tbsp hot sauce
- 1 oz cheddar cheese, shredded
- 1 oz parmesan cheese, shredded
- 1/4 cup breadcrumbs
- Pepper
- Salt

Directions:

1. Add all ingredients into the bowl and mix until well combined.
2. Spray air fryer basket with cooking spray.
3. Make patties from the mixture and place into the air fryer basket and cook at 400 F for 10 minutes.
4. Serve and enjoy.

Nutritional Value (Amount per Serving):

- Calories 167
- Fat 8.4 g
- Carbohydrates 6.2 g
- Sugar 0.9 g
- Protein 16.3 g
- Cholesterol 65 mg

Tasty Tuna Steaks

Preparation Time: 10 minutes
Cooking Time: 10 minutes
Serve: 2

Ingredients:

- 1 lb tuna
- 1 tbsp garlic, minced
- 4 tbsp olive oil
- 1 tbsp garlic powder
- 1/2 tsp thyme
- Pepper
- Salt

Directions:

1. In a bowl, mix oil, garlic, garlic powder, thyme, pepper, and salt. Add tuna steaks and mix well and place in the refrigerator for 15 minutes.
2. Place tuna steaks into the air fryer basket and cook at 400 F for 10 minutes.
3. Serve and enjoy.

Nutritional Value (Amount per Serving):

- Calories 683
- Fat 46.4 g
- Carbohydrates 4.6 g
- Sugar 1.1 g
- Protein 61.2 g
- Cholesterol 70 mg

Flavorful Tuna Patties

Preparation Time: 10 minutes
Cooking Time: 10 minutes
Serve: 8

Ingredients:

- 2 eggs
- 10 oz can tuna, chopped
- 2 tbsp mayonnaise
- 1/2 tsp garlic powder
- 1/4 cup fresh mint, chopped
- 1/4 cup feta cheese, crumbled
- 1/2 onion, chopped
- Pepper
- Salt

Directions:

1. Add all ingredients into the bowl and mix until well combined.
2. Spray air fryer basket with cooking spray.
3. Make patties from the mixture and place into the air fryer basket and cook at 400 F for 10 minutes.
4. Serve and enjoy.

Nutritional Value (Amount per Serving):

- Calories 88
- Fat 3.6 g
- Carbohydrates 2.2 g
- Sugar 0.8 g
- Protein 11.3 g
- Cholesterol 57 mg

BBQ Salmon

Preparation Time: 10 minutes
Cooking Time: 25 minutes
Serve: 4

Ingredients:

- 4 salmon fillets
- For sauce:
- 2 tsp soy sauce
- 3 tbsp balsamic vinegar
- 3 tbsp brown sugar
- 1 cup tomato ketchup
- Pepper
- Salt

Directions:

1. Add all sauce ingredients into the small saucepan and bring to boil over medium heat. Turn heat to low and simmer for 15 minutes.
2. Spray salmon fillets with cooking spray and season with pepper and salt.
3. Place salmon fillets into the air fryer basket and cook at 380 for 5 minutes.
4. Brush salmon fillets with BBQ sauce and cook for 5 minutes more.
5. Serve and enjoy.

Nutritional Value (Amount per Serving):

- Calories 323
- Fat 11.2 g
- Carbohydrates 22 g
- Sugar 20.3 g
- Protein 35.8 g
- Cholesterol 78 mg

Crispy Coconut Shrimp

Preparation Time: 10 minutes
Cooking Time: 5 minutes
Serve: 4

Ingredients:

- 2 eggs, lightly beaten
- 20 large shrimp, peeled
- 1/4 cup whole-wheat breadcrumbs
- 1/2 cup shredded coconut
- 1/4 tsp garlic powder
- 1/2 cup all-purpose flour
- Pepper
- Salt

Directions:

1. In a small bowl, add eggs and whisk well.
2. In a shallow dish, mix breadcrumbs, shredded coconut, garlic powder, flour, pepper, and salt.
3. Preheat the air fryer to 400 F.
4. Dip shrimp in egg then coat with breadcrumb mixture.
5. Spray air fryer basket with cooking spray.
6. Place shrimp into the air fryer basket and cook for 5 minutes.
7. Serve and enjoy.

Nutritional Value (Amount per Serving):

- Calories 184
- Fat 6.5 g
- Carbohydrates 19.1 g
- Sugar 1.3 g
- Protein 11.9 g
- Cholesterol 140 mg

Tasty Shrimp Fajitas

Preparation Time: 10 minutes
Cooking Time: 9 minutes
Serve: 4

Ingredients:

- 1 lb shrimp, thawed
- 3/4 tbsp Fajita seasoning
- 1 tbsp olive oil
- 1 small onion, sliced
- 3 small bell peppers, sliced
- Pepper
- Salt

Directions:

1. Preheat the air fryer to 375 F.
2. Add shrimp and remaining ingredients into the bowl and toss well.
3. Add shrimp mixture into the air fryer basket and cook for 9 minutes. Stir halfway through.
4. Serve and enjoy.

Nutritional Value (Amount per Serving):

- Calories 206
- Fat 5.7 g
- Carbohydrates 11.3 g
- Sugar 5.2 g
- Protein 26.9 g
- Cholesterol 239 mg

Garlic Honey Shrimp

Preparation Time: 10 minutes
Cooking Time: 10 minutes
Serve: 6

Ingredients:

- 16 oz shrimp, peeled & deveined
- 16 oz mixed vegetables
- 2 tbsp cornstarch
- 1 tsp ginger garlic paste
- 2 tbsp ketchup
- 1/2 cup soy sauce
- 1/2 cup honey

Directions:

1. Add soy sauce, ketchup, ginger garlic paste, and honey into the small saucepan and cook over medium heat until warm.
2. Add cornstarch and stir constantly until thickened.
3. Remove saucepan from heat. Pour sauce over shrimp and vegetables and toss well.
4. Preheat the air fryer to 350 F.
5. Spray air fryer basket with cooking spray.
6. Add shrimp and vegetables into the air fryer basket and cook for 10 minutes.
7. Serve and enjoy.

Nutritional Value (Amount per Serving):

- Calories 229
- Fat 1.5 g
- Carbohydrates 35.1 g
- Sugar 24.7 g
- Protein 19.8 g
- Cholesterol 159 mg

Delicious Fish Bites

Preparation Time: 10 minutes
Cooking Time: 10 minutes
Serve: 4

Ingredients:

- 1 egg, lightly beaten
- 1 lb cod fillets, cut into 1-inch strips
- 1/2 tsp lemon pepper seasoning
- 1/2 tsp smoked paprika
- 1/2 cup whole-wheat breadcrumbs
- 1/2 cup all-purpose flour
- Pepper
- Salt

Directions:

1. In a small bowl, add egg and whisk well.
2. In a separate bowl, mix flour, pepper, and salt.
3. In a shallow dish, mix breadcrumbs, paprika, and lemon pepper seasoning.
4. Coat fish strips with flour then dip in egg and finally coat with breadcrumb mixture.
5. Preheat the air fryer to 400 F.
6. Spray air fryer basket with cooking spray.
7. Place coated fish strips into the air fryer basket and cook for 10 minutes. Turn fish strips halfway through.
8. Serve and enjoy.

Nutritional Value (Amount per Serving):

- Calories 234
- Fat 2 g
- Carbohydrates 37.7 g
- Sugar 0.2 g
- Protein 16.4 g
- Cholesterol 61 mg

Garlic Cheese Shrimp

Preparation Time: 10 minutes
Cooking Time: 8 minutes
Serve: 6

Ingredients:

- 2 lbs cooked shrimp, peeled & deveined
- 2 tbsp olive oil
- 3/4 tsp onion powder
- 1 tsp basil
- 1/2 tsp oregano
- 2/3 cup parmesan cheese, grated
- 1 tbsp garlic, minced
- Pepper
- Salt

Directions:

1. Add shrimp and remaining ingredients into the bowl and toss until well coated.
2. Add shrimp into the air fryer basket and cook at 350 F for 8 minutes.
3. Serve and enjoy.

Nutritional Value (Amount per Serving):

- Calories 223
- Fat 7.3 g
- Carbohydrates 3.1 g
- Sugar 0.1 g
- Protein 34.6 g
- Cholesterol 318 mg

Crispy Shrimp Popcorn

Preparation Time: 10 minutes
Cooking Time: 5 minutes
Serve: 4

Ingredients:

- 2 eggs, lightly beaten
- 5 oz oat flour
- 2 oz parmesan cheese, grated
- 8 oz whole-wheat breadcrumbs
- 1 lb shrimp, cooked & peeled
- Pepper
- Salt

Directions:

1. In a small bowl, add eggs and whisk well.
2. In a separate bowl, add oat flour.
3. In a shallow dish, mix breadcrumbs, cheese, pepper, and salt.
4. Coat shrimp with oat flour then dip in eggs and finally coat with breadcrumb mixture.
5. Place coated shrimp into the air fryer basket and cook at 400 F for 5 minutes.
6. Serve and enjoy.

Nutritional Value (Amount per Serving):

- Calories 356
- Fat 9.6 g
- Carbohydrates 27.6 g
- Sugar 0.2 g
- Protein 37.9 g
- Cholesterol 331 mg

Lemon Garlic Shrimp

Preparation Time: 10 minutes
Cooking Time: 8 minutes
Serve: 4

Ingredients:

- 1 lb shrimp, peeled & deveined
- 2 tbsp parmesan cheese, grated
- 1/2 tsp garlic, minced
- 1 tsp lemon juice
- 1 tbsp butter, melted
- Salt

Directions:

1. Add shrimp and remaining ingredients into the bowl and toss well.
2. Add shrimp mixture into the air fryer basket and cook at 400 F for 8 minutes.
3. Serve and enjoy.

Nutritional Value (Amount per Serving):

- Calories 161
- Fat 4.8 g
- Carbohydrates 1.9 g
- Sugar 0 g
- Protein 25.9 g
- Cholesterol 246 mg

Shrimp Boil

Preparation Time: 10 minutes
Cooking Time: 12 minutes
Serve: 4

Ingredients:

- 6 oz shrimp, peeled & deveined
- 1 tbsp old bay seasoning
- 2 tbsp onion, diced
- 2 mini corn on the cobs
- 2 cups baby potatoes, boiled & halved
- 7 oz smoked sausage, sliced

Directions:

1. Add shrimp and remaining ingredients into the bowl and toss well.
2. Add shrimp mixture into the air fryer basket and cook for 12 minutes. Mix halfway through.
3. Stir well and serve.

Nutritional Value (Amount per Serving):

- Calories 221
- Fat 14.8 g
- Carbohydrates 1.1 g
- Sugar 0.2 g
- Protein 19.4 g
- Cholesterol 131 mg

Crispy Salt & Pepper Shrimp

Preparation Time: 10 minutes

Cooking Time: 10 minutes

Serve: 4

Ingredients:

- 1 lb shrimp
- 2 tbsp olive oil
- 3 tbsp rice flour
- 1 tsp sugar, crushed
- 2 tsp ground pepper
- Salt

Directions:

1. Add shrimp, oil, rice flour, sugar, pepper, and salt into the bowl and toss well.
2. Spray air fryer basket with cooking spray.
3. Add shrimp into the air fryer basket and cook at 325 F for 10 minutes.
4. Serve and enjoy.

Nutritional Value (Amount per Serving):

- Calories 228
- Fat 9.1 g
- Carbohydrates 9.3 g
- Sugar 1 g
- Protein 26.4 g
- Cholesterol 239 mg

Asian Shrimp

Preparation Time: 10 minutes
Cooking Time: 6 minutes
Serve: 4

Ingredients:

- 1 lb shrimp, peeled & deveined
- For marinade:
- 1 tbsp lemon juice
- 1 tsp garlic, minced
- 1/8 tsp cayenne
- 1 tbsp maple syrup
- 2 tbsp soy sauce
- 2 tbsp olive oil
- Pepper
- Salt

Directions:

1. Add shrimp and marinade ingredients into the bowl and mix well and place in the refrigerator for 15 minutes.
2. Spray air fryer basket with cooking spray.
3. Place shrimp into the air fryer basket and cook at 400 F for 6 minutes.
4. Serve and enjoy.

Nutritional Value (Amount per Serving):

- Calories 214
- Fat 9 g
- Carbohydrates 6 g
- Sugar 3.2 g
- Protein 26.4 g
- Cholesterol 239 mg

Flavorful Blackened Shrimp

Preparation Time: 10 minutes
Cooking Time: 10 minutes
Serve: 4

Ingredients:

- 1 lb shrimp, peeled & deveined
- 2 tsp smoked paprika
- 1/4 tsp cayenne
- 1 tsp dried oregano
- 1 tsp garlic powder
- 1 tsp onion powder
- 2 tbsp olive oil
- Pepper
- Salt

Directions:

1. Add shrimp and remaining ingredients into the bowl and toss well.
2. Preheat the air fryer to 400 F.
3. Spray air fryer basket with cooking spray.
4. Add shrimp into the air fryer basket and cook for 8-10 minutes or until cooked through.
5. Serve and enjoy.

Nutritional Value (Amount per Serving):

- Calories 204
- Fat 9.1 g
- Carbohydrates 3.6 g
- Sugar 0.5 g
- Protein 26.2 g
- Cholesterol 239 mg

Shrimp Dinner

Preparation Time: 10 minutes
Cooking Time: 8 minutes
Serve: 4

Ingredients:

- 1 lb shrimp, peeled
- 2 tbsp olive oil
- 1 bell pepper, cut into 1-inch pieces
- 1 squash, cut into slices
- 1 zucchini, cut into slices
- 6 oz sausage, sliced
- 1 tbsp Cajun seasoning
- Salt

Directions:

1. Preheat the air fryer to 400 F.
2. Add shrimp and remaining ingredients into the bowl and toss well.
3. Add shrimp mixture into the air fryer basket and cook for 8 minutes.
4. Serve and enjoy.

Nutritional Value (Amount per Serving):

- Calories 364
- Fat 21.2 g
- Carbohydrates 7.3 g
- Sugar 3.2 g
- Protein 35.6 g
- Cholesterol 275 mg

Shrimp with Veggie

Preparation Time: 10 minutes
Cooking Time: 15 minutes
Serve: 4

Ingredients:

- 1 lb shrimp, peeled & deveined
- 1/4 cup parmesan cheese, grated
- 1 tbsp Italian seasoning
- 1 tbsp garlic, minced
- 1 tbsp olive oil
- 1 bell pepper, chopped
- 1 zucchini, chopped
- Pepper
- Salt

Directions:

1. Add shrimp and remaining ingredients into the bowl and toss well.
2. Add shrimp mixture into the air fryer basket and cook at 390 F for 15 minutes. Stir halfway through.
3. Serve and enjoy.

Nutritional Value (Amount per Serving):

- Calories 196
- Fat 6.6 g
- Carbohydrates 6.7 g
- Sugar 2.7 g
- Protein 26.9 g
- Cholesterol 241 mg

Perfect Shrimp Skewers

Preparation Time: 10 minutes
Cooking Time: 8 minutes
Serve: 4

Ingredients:

- 1/2 lb shrimp, peeled & deveined
- 1 tbsp cilantro, chopped
- 1 lemon juice
- 1/2 tsp ground cumin
- 1/2 tsp smoked paprika
- 1/2 tsp garlic paste
- Salt

Directions:

1. Add shrimp and remaining ingredients into the bowl and mix well. Cover and place in the refrigerator for 15 minutes.
2. Thread shrimp onto the soaked skewers.
3. Preheat the air fryer to 350 F.
4. Place shrimp skewers into the air fryer basket and cook for 8 minutes.
5. Serve and enjoy.

Nutritional Value (Amount per Serving):

- Calories 70
- Fat 1.1 g
- Carbohydrates 1.3 g
- Sugar 0 g
- Protein 13 g
- Cholesterol 119 mg

Shrimp with Onion & Pepper

Preparation Time: 10 minutes
Cooking Time: 15 minutes
Serve: 4

Ingredients:

- 1 lb shrimp, peeled & deveined
- 1/8 tsp cayenne
- 1/2 tsp garlic powder
- 1 tsp chili powder
- 1 tbsp olive oil
- 1/2 onion, cut into chunks
- 1 bell pepper, cut into chunks
- Pepper
- Salt

Directions:

1. Add shrimp and remaining ingredients into the bowl and toss well.
2. Add shrimp mixture into the air fryer basket and cook at 330 F for 15 minutes. Stir halfway through.
3. Serve and enjoy.

Nutritional Value (Amount per Serving):

- Calories 183
- Fat 5.6 g
- Carbohydrates 5.9 g
- Sugar 2.2 g
- Protein 26.4 g
- Cholesterol 239 mg

Hawaiian Shrimp

Preparation Time: 10 minutes
Cooking Time: 8 minutes
Serve: 4

Ingredients:

- 1 lb shrimp
- 1 1/2 tsp paprika
- 2 tbsp cornstarch
- 1 tbsp garlic, minced
- 1/4 cup butter
- Pepper
- Salt

Directions:

1. Add shrimp, cornstarch, paprika, pepper, and salt into the bowl and toss until well coated.
2. Spray air fryer basket with cooking spray.
3. Add shrimp into the air fryer basket and cook at 350 F for 8 minutes.
4. Melt butter in a pan over medium heat, once butter is melted then add garlic and sauté for 30 seconds.
5. Pour garlic butter mixture over shrimp and serve.

Nutritional Value (Amount per Serving):

- Calories 257
- Fat 13.5 g
- Carbohydrates 6.5 g
- Sugar 0.1 g
- Protein 26.2 g
- Cholesterol 269 mg

Lemon Old Bay Shrimp

Preparation Time: 10 minutes
Cooking Time: 10 minutes
Serve: 4

Ingredients:

- 1 lb shrimp, peeled & deveined
- 1 tbsp old bay seasoning
- 1/2 tsp garlic, minced
- 1/2 tsp lemon juice
- 1/2 tbsp butter, melted
- Pepper
- Salt

Directions:

1. Add shrimp and remaining ingredients into the bowl and toss well.
2. Add shrimp mixture into the air fryer basket and cook at 390 F for 8-10 minutes. Stir halfway through.
3. Serve and enjoy.

Nutritional Value (Amount per Serving):

- Calories 148
- Fat 3.4 g
- Carbohydrates 1.9 g
- Sugar 0 g
- Protein 25.9 g
- Cholesterol 243 mg

Southwest Shrimp

Preparation Time: 10 minutes
Cooking Time: 6 minutes
Serve: 4

Ingredients:

- 1 lb shrimp, peeled & deveined
- 1 1/2 tsp southwestern seasoning
- 1 tsp butter, melted

Directions:

1. In a bowl, toss shrimp with seasoning and melted butter.
2. Preheat the air fryer to 400 F.
3. Add shrimp into the air fryer basket and cook for 6 minutes.
4. Serve and enjoy.

Nutritional Value (Amount per Serving):

- Calories 143
- Fat 2.9 g
- Carbohydrates 1.7 g
- Sugar 0 g
- Protein 25.8 g
- Cholesterol 241 mg

Easy Spicy Shrimp

Preparation Time: 10 minutes
Cooking Time: 7 minutes
Serve: 4

Ingredients:

- 1 lb shrimp
- 1/4 tsp ground mustard
- 1/4 tsp ground cumin
- 1/4 tsp oregano
- 1/4 tsp thyme
- 1/4 tsp cayenne
- 1/4 tsp garlic powder
- 1/2 tsp paprika
- 1 tsp chili powder
- 1 tsp olive oil
- Pepper
- Salt

Directions:

1. Preheat the air fryer to 400 F.
2. Add shrimp and remaining ingredients into the bowl and toss well.
3. Add shrimp mixture into the air fryer basket and cook for 7 minutes. Stir halfway through.
4. Serve and enjoy.

Nutritional Value (Amount per Serving):

- Calories 150
- Fat 3.4 g
- Carbohydrates 2.7 g
- Sugar 0.1 g
- Protein 26.1 g
- Cholesterol 239 mg

Perfect Air Fried Shrimp

Preparation Time: 10 minutes
Cooking Time: 8 minutes
Serve: 4

Ingredients:

- 1 lb shrimp
- 1/2 tsp Italian seasoning
- 1/4 tsp paprika
- 1/2 tsp garlic powder
- 2 tsp olive oil
- Pepper
- Salt

Directions:

1. Preheat the air fryer to 400 F.
2. Add shrimp and remaining ingredients into the bowl and toss well.
3. Add shrimp mixture into the air fryer basket and cook for 8 minutes.
4. Serve and enjoy.

Nutritional Value (Amount per Serving):

- Calories 158
- Fat 4.4 g
- Carbohydrates 2.1 g
- Sugar 0.2 g
- Protein 25.9 g
- Cholesterol 239 mg

Healthy Cod Fish Fillets

Preparation Time: 10 minutes
Cooking Time: 10 minutes
Serve: 4

Ingredients:

- 2 eggs
- 1 tsp garlic powder
- 1 tsp lemon pepper seasoning
- 1 cup parmesan cheese, grated
- 1 cup almond flour
- 1/2 cup whole-wheat breadcrumbs
- 1/4 cup all-purpose flour
- 4 cod fillets
- Pepper
- Salt

Directions:

1. In a small bowl, whisk eggs with pepper and salt.
2. In a shallow dish, mix breadcrumbs, almond flour, cheese, lemon pepper seasoning, and garlic powder.
3. In a separate bowl, add flour.
4. Coat fish fillets with flour then dip in the egg mixture and finally coat with breadcrumb mixture.
5. Place coated fish fillets into the air fryer basket and cook at 350 F for 8-10 minutes.
6. Serve and enjoy.

Nutritional Value (Amount per Serving):

- Calories 64
- Fat 2.3 g
- Carbohydrates 7 g
- Sugar 0.4 g
- Protein 3.8 g
- Cholesterol 82 mg

Flavorful Salmon Steak

Preparation Time: 10 minutes
Cooking Time: 14 minutes
Serve: 2

Ingredients:

- 2 salmon steaks
- 2 tsp ground sage
- 4 tbsp butter, melted
- Pepper
- Salt

Directions:

1. In a small bowl, mix butter, sage, pepper, and salt.
2. Brush salmon steaks with butter mixture and place into the air fryer basket and cook at 400 F for 14 minutes.
3. Serve and enjoy.

Nutritional Value (Amount per Serving):

- Calories 441
- Fat 34.1 g
- Carbohydrates 0.5 g
- Sugar 0 g
- Protein 34.9 g
- Cholesterol 140 mg

Honey Garlic Shrimp Skewers

Preparation Time: 10 minutes
Cooking Time: 5 minutes
Serve: 4

Ingredients:

- 1 lb shrimp
- 2 tsp garlic, minced
- 2 tbsp olive oil
- 3 tbsp soy sauce
- 1/2 cup honey

Directions:

1. Add shrimp, garlic, oil, soy sauce, and honey into the bowl and mix well. Cover and place in the refrigerator for overnight.
2. Thread marinated shrimp onto the soaked wooden skewers.
3. Place shrimp skewers into the air fryer basket and cook at 400 F for 5 minutes.
4. Serve and enjoy.

Nutritional Value (Amount per Serving):

- Calories 332
- Fat 8.9 g
- Carbohydrates 38 g
- Sugar 35 g
- Protein 26.8 g
- Cholesterol 239 mg

Flavorful Spicy Shrimp

Preparation Time: 10 minutes
Cooking Time: 10 minutes
Serve: 4

Ingredients:

- 2 lb shrimp, peeled & deveined
- 1 tbsp lemon juice
- 2 tbsp soy sauce
- 1 tsp garlic powder
- 1 tsp sugar
- 1 tsp ground cumin
- 1 tsp liquid smoke
- 1 tsp chili powder
- 1 tbsp Tabasco sauce
- 1 tsp paprika
- Pepper
- Salt

Directions:

1. Add shrimp and remaining ingredients into the bowl and toss well.
2. Add shrimp mixture into the air fryer basket and cook at 400 F for 10 minutes. Stir halfway through.
3. Serve and enjoy.

Nutritional Value (Amount per Serving):

- Calories 287
- Fat 4.2 g
- Carbohydrates 6.6 g
- Sugar 1.5 g
- Protein 52.6 g
- Cholesterol 478 mg

Scallops with Sauce

Preparation Time: 10 minutes

Cooking Time: 7 minutes

Serve: 4

Ingredients:

- 1 lb sea scallops
- 2 tsp garlic, minced
- 3 tbsp heavy cream
- 1/4 cup pesto
- 1 tbsp olive oil
- Pepper
- Salt

Directions:

1. Season scallops with pepper and salt.
2. Place scallops into the air fryer basket and cook at 320 F for 5 minutes.
3. In a pan, add cream, pesto, oil, and garlic and cook for 2 minutes.
4. Pour sauce over cooked scallops and serve.

Nutritional Value (Amount per Serving):

- Calories 238
- Fat 15 g
- Carbohydrates 4.5 g
- Sugar 1 g
- Protein 20.9 g
- Cholesterol 57 mg

Tasty Tuna Cakes

Preparation Time: 10 minutes
Cooking Time: 6 minutes
Serve: 4

Ingredients:

- 1 egg
- 7 oz can tuna
- 1/4 cup whole-wheat breadcrumbs
- 1 tbsp mustard
- Pepper
- Salt

Directions:

1. Add all ingredients into the bowl and mix until well combined.
2. Make patties from the mixture and place into the air fryer basket and cook at 400 F for 6 minutes. Turn patties halfway through.
3. Serve and enjoy.

Nutritional Value (Amount per Serving):

- Calories 113
- Fat 2.7 g
- Carbohydrates 5.9 g
- Sugar 0.7 g
- Protein 15.6 g
- Cholesterol 56 mg

Easy Salmon Patties

Preparation Time: 10 minutes
Cooking Time: 10 minutes
Serve: 4

Ingredients:

- 1 egg
- 1 tsp dill weed
- 1/2 cup whole-wheat breadcrumbs
- 1/4 cup onion, chopped
- 14 oz can salmon, remove bones & skin
- Pepper
- Salt

Directions:

1. Add all ingredients into the bowl and mix until well combined.
2. Make patties from the mixture and place into the air fryer basket and cook at 370 F for 10 minutes. Turn patties halfway through.
3. Serve and enjoy.

Nutritional Value (Amount per Serving):

- Calories 157
- Fat 7.1 g
- Carbohydrates 0.9 g
- Sugar 0.4 g
- Protein 21.1 g
- Cholesterol 95 mg

Quick & Easy Scallops

Preparation Time: 10 minutes
Cooking Time: 4 minutes
Serve: 2

Ingredients:

- 8 scallops
- 1 tsp olive oil
- Pepper
- Salt

Directions:

1. Preheat the air fryer to 390 F.
2. Add scallops, oil, pepper, and salt into the bowl and toss well.
3. Add scallops into the air fryer basket and cook for 4 minutes. Turn scallops halfway through.
4. Serve and enjoy.

Nutritional Value (Amount per Serving):

- Calories 126
- Fat 3.2 g
- Carbohydrates 2.9 g
- Sugar 0 g
- Protein 20.2 g
- Cholesterol 40 mg

Cajun Scallops

Preparation Time: 10 minutes
Cooking Time: 6 minutes
Serve: 2

Ingredients:

- 6 scallops
- 1/2 tsp Cajun seasoning
- 1 tsp olive oil
- Salt

Directions:

1. Preheat the air fryer to 400 F.
2. Add scallops, oil, Cajun seasoning, and salt into the bowl and toss well.
3. Add scallops into the air fryer basket and cook for 6 minutes. Turn scallops halfway through.
4. Serve and enjoy.

Nutritional Value (Amount per Serving):

- Calories 99
- Fat 3 g
- Carbohydrates 2.1 g
- Sugar 0 g
- Protein 15.1 g
- Cholesterol 30 mg

Creamy Scallops

Preparation Time: 10 minutes
Cooking Time: 10 minutes
Serve: 4

Ingredients:

- 1 lb sea scallops
- 1 tbsp white wine
- 1 tsp garlic, minced
- 2 tsp lemon juice
- 3 tbsp heavy cream
- 3 tbsp butter
- Pepper
- Salt

Directions:

1. Preheat the air fryer to 400 F.
2. Season scallops with pepper and salt and place into the air fryer basket and cook for 10 minutes. Turn scallops halfway through.
3. Melt butter in a pan over medium heat.
4. Add garlic and sauté for 30 seconds. Add wine, lemon juice, and heavy cream and stir until thickened.
5. Pour sauce over cooked scallops and serve.

Nutritional Value (Amount per Serving):

- Calories 220
- Fat 13.7 g
- Carbohydrates 3.4 g
- Sugar 0.1 g
- Protein 19.4 g
- Cholesterol 76 mg

Flavors Crab Cakes

Preparation Time: 10 minutes
Cooking Time: 12 minutes
Serve: 4

Ingredients:

- 1 egg
- 1 lb crab meat
- 1 tbsp capers
- 1 roasted red pepper, diced
- 2 green onions, chopped
- 2/3 cup whole-wheat breadcrumbs
- 1 tbsp parsley, chopped
- 1/2 lemon juice
- 2 tsp old bay seasoning
- 1 tbsp soy sauce
- 1 tbsp Dijon mustard
- 1/4 cup mayonnaise
- Salt

Directions:

1. Preheat the air fryer to 360 F.
2. Spray air fryer basket with cooking spray.
3. Add all ingredients into the mixing bowl and mix until well combined.
4. Make the equal shape of patties from the mixture and place into the air fryer basket and cook for 7 minutes.
5. Flip patties and cook for 5 minutes more.
6. Serve and enjoy.

Nutritional Value (Amount per Serving):

- Calories 187
- Fat 8.3 g
- Carbohydrates 8 g
- Sugar 2.1 g
- Protein 16.5 g
- Cholesterol 105 mg

Quick & Easy Salmon Patties

Preparation Time: 10 minutes
Cooking Time: 8 minutes
Serve: 6

Ingredients:

- 1 egg
- 1 tsp paprika
- 2 green onions, minced
- 2 tbsp fresh coriander, chopped
- 14 oz can salmon, drain & remove bones
- Salt

Directions:

1. Preheat the air fryer to 360 F.
2. Add all ingredients into the mixing bowl and mix until well combined.
3. Make the equal shape of patties from the mixture and place into the air fryer basket and cook for 8 minutes.
4. Serve and enjoy.

Nutritional Value (Amount per Serving):

- Calories 105
- Fat 4.8 g
- Carbohydrates 0.6 g
- Sugar 0.2 g
- Protein 14.2 g
- Cholesterol 64 mg

Healthy Salmon Patties

Preparation Time: 10 minutes
Cooking Time: 15 minutes
Serve: 4

Ingredients:

- 2 eggs, lightly beaten
- 2 oz salmon, cooked & flaked
- 2 tsp nutritional yeast
- 1/4 tsp paprika
- 1 tsp garlic, minced
- 1/4 cup onion, diced
- 2/3 cup almond flour
- Pepper
- Salt

Directions:

1. Preheat the air fryer to 380 F.
2. Add all ingredients into the mixing bowl and mix until well combined.
3. Make the equal shape of patties from the mixture and place into the air fryer basket and cook for 12-15 minutes.
4. Serve and enjoy.

Nutritional Value (Amount per Serving):

- Calories 60
- Fat 3.2 g
- Carbohydrates 1.9 g
- Sugar 0.5 g
- Protein 6.4 g
- Cholesterol 88 mg

Cheesy Salmon

Preparation Time: 10 minutes
Cooking Time: 7 minutes
Serve: 4

Ingredients:

- 4 salmon fillets
- 1/4 cup parmesan cheese, grated
- 3 tbsp mayonnaise
- Pepper
- Salt

Directions:

1. Preheat the air fryer to 400 F.
2. Spray air fryer basket with cooking spray.
3. In a bowl, mix cheese, mayonnaise, pepper, and salt.
4. Spread cheese mixture on top of fish fillets.
5. Place fish fillets into the air fryer basket and cook for 7 minutes.
6. Serve and enjoy.

Nutritional Value (Amount per Serving):

- Calories 279
- Fat 14.7 g
- Carbohydrates 2.7 g
- Sugar 0.7 g
- Protein 34.6 g
- Cholesterol 81 mg

Tasty Pesto Salmon

Preparation Time: 10 minutes
Cooking Time: 15 minutes
Serve: 4

Ingredients:

- 4 salmon fillets
- 1 tbsp olive oil
- 1/4 cup pesto

Directions:

1. Preheat the air fryer to 360 F.
2. Spray air fryer basket with cooking spray.
3. Place salmon fillets into the air fryer basket. Mix pesto and oil and spread on top of salmon fillets.
4. Cook salmon fillets for 12-15 minutes.
5. Serve and enjoy.

Nutritional Value (Amount per Serving):

- Calories 333
- Fat 21 g
- Carbohydrates 1 g
- Sugar 1 g
- Protein 36 g
- Cholesterol 82 mg

Everything Bagel Salmon

Preparation Time: 10 minutes
Cooking Time: 12 minutes
Serve: 2

Ingredients:

- 2 salmon fillets
- 4 tbsp everything bagel seasoning
- 2 tbsp olive oil

Directions:

1. Preheat the air fryer to 350 F.
2. Spray air fryer basket with cooking spray.
3. Brush salmon fillets with oil and coat with bagel seasoning.
4. Place fish fillets into the air fryer basket and cook for 12 minutes.
5. Serve and enjoy.

Nutritional Value (Amount per Serving):

- Calories 355
- Fat 25 g
- Carbohydrates 0 g
- Sugar 0 g
- Protein 34.5 g
- Cholesterol 78 mg

Pesto White Fish Fillets

Preparation Time: 10 minutes
Cooking Time: 8 minutes
Serve: 2

Ingredients:

- 2 white fish fillets
- 1 tbsp olive oil
- 1/4 cup basil pesto

Directions:

1. Preheat the air fryer to 360 F.
2. Spray air fryer basket with cooking spray.
3. Place fish fillets into the air fryer basket. Mix pesto and oil and spread on top of fish fillets.
4. Cook fish fillets for 8 minutes.
5. Serve and enjoy.

Nutritional Value (Amount per Serving):

- Calories 326
- Fat 18.6 g
- Carbohydrates 0.1 g
- Sugar 0 g
- Protein 37.8 g
- Cholesterol 119 mg

Bagel Crust White Fish Fillets

Preparation Time: 10 minutes
Cooking Time: 10 minutes
Serve: 4

Ingredients:

- 4 white fish fillets
- 1 tbsp mayonnaise
- 1 tsp lemon pepper seasoning
- 2 tbsp almond flour
- 4 tbsp everything bagel seasoning

Directions:

1. Preheat the air fryer to 375 F.
2. In a shallow dish, mix almond flour, lemon pepper seasoning, and bagel seasoning.
3. Brush fish fillets with mayonnaise and coat with almond flour mixture.
4. Place fish fillets into the air fryer basket and cook for 8-10 minutes.
5. Serve and enjoy.

Nutritional Value (Amount per Serving):

- Calories 281
- Fat 12.8 g
- Carbohydrates 1.2 g
- Sugar 0.2 g
- Protein 37.8 g
- Cholesterol 120 mg

Parmesan White Fish Fillets

Preparation Time: 10 minutes
Cooking Time: 15 minutes
Serve: 2

Ingredients:

- 2 white fish fillets
- 1/2 tsp paprika
- 1/2 tsp onion powder
- 1/2 tsp garlic powder
- 1/2 cup parmesan cheese, grated
- 1 tbsp olive oil
- Pepper
- Salt

Directions:

1. Preheat the air fryer to 380 F.
2. In a shallow dish, mix cheese, garlic powder, onion powder, paprika, pepper, and salt.
3. Brush fish fillets with oil and coat with cheese mixture.
4. Spray air fryer basket with cooking spray.
5. Place coated fish fillets into the air fryer basket and cook for 12-15 minutes.
6. Serve and enjoy.

Nutritional Value (Amount per Serving):

- Calories 331
- Fat 18.7 g
- Carbohydrates 1.3 g
- Sugar 0.4 g
- Protein 38 g
- Cholesterol 119 mg

Chapter 4: Vegetable & Side Dishes

Healthy Mix Vegetables

Preparation Time: 10 minutes

Cooking Time: 18 minutes

Serve: 4

Ingredients:

- 1 cup broccoli florets
- 1 cup carrots, sliced
- 1 cup cauliflower, cut into florets
- ¼ tsp garlic powder
- 1 tbsp olive oil
- Pepper
- Salt

Directions:

1. Add all ingredients into the bowl and toss well.
2. Add vegetable mixture into the air fryer basket and cook at 380 F for 18 minutes. Stir halfway through.
3. Serve and enjoy.

Nutritional Value (Amount per Serving):

- Calories 56
- Fat 3.6 g
- Carbohydrates 5.6 g
- Sugar 2.3 g
- Protein 1.4 g
- Cholesterol 0 mg

Healthy Asparagus

Preparation Time: 10 minutes
Cooking Time: 7 minutes
Serve: 4

Ingredients:

- 1 lb asparagus, cut the ends
- 1 tsp butter, melted
- Pepper
- Salt

Directions:

1. Preheat the air fryer to 350 F.
2. Add asparagus, butter, pepper, and salt into the bowl and toss well.
3. Add asparagus into the air fryer basket and cook for 7 minutes.
4. Serve and enjoy.

Nutritional Value (Amount per Serving):

- Calories 35
- Fat 1.3 g
- Carbohydrates 4.4 g
- Sugar 2.1 g
- Protein 2.5 g
- Cholesterol 0 mg

Garlic Cheese Broccoli

Preparation Time: 10 minutes
Cooking Time: 5 minutes
Serve: 4

Ingredients:

- 1 lb broccoli florets
- 2 tbsp butter, melted
- ¼ tsp chili flakes, crushed
- ¼ cup parmesan cheese, grated
- 1 tbsp garlic, minced
- Pepper
- Salt

Directions:

1. Preheat the air fryer to 350 F.
2. Add broccoli and remaining ingredients into the bowl and toss well.
3. Add broccoli mixture into the air fryer basket and cook for 5 minutes.
4. Serve and enjoy.

Nutritional Value (Amount per Serving):

- Calories 250
- Fat 16.4 g
- Carbohydrates 8.2 g
- Sugar 2 g
- Protein 15.3 g
- Cholesterol 30 mg

Hassel-back Potatoes

Preparation Time: 10 minutes
Cooking Time: 20 minutes
Serve: 4

Ingredients:

- 4 potatoes, wash and dry
- ½ cup butter, melted
- Pepper
- Salt

Directions:

1. Preheat the air fryer to 325 F.
2. Place potato in Hassel back slicer and slice potato using a sharp knife.
3. Brush potatoes with butter and season with pepper and salt.
4. Place potatoes into the air fryer basket and cook for 20 minutes.
5. Serve and enjoy.

Nutritional Value (Amount per Serving):

- Calories 355
- Fat 23.4 g
- Carbohydrates 34.5 g
- Sugar 2.5 g
- Protein 4 g
- Cholesterol 61 mg

Zucchini Carrot Tots

Preparation Time: 10 minutes
Cooking Time: 10 minutes
Serve: 2

Ingredients:

- 1 egg
- 1 carrot, grated & squeeze out the liquid
- 1/4 cup breadcrumbs
- 1 zucchini, grated & squeeze out the liquid
- 1/4 cup parmesan cheese, grated
- ¼ tsp garlic powder
- Pepper
- Salt

Directions:

1. Preheat the air fryer to 400 F.
2. Spray air fryer basket with cooking spray.
3. Add all ingredients into the bowl and mix until well combined.
4. Make tots from mixture and place into the air fryer basket and cook for 10 minutes.
5. Serve and enjoy.

Nutritional Value (Amount per Serving):

- Calories 150
- Fat 5.5 g
- Carbohydrates 16.6 g
- Sugar 4.2 g
- Protein 9.6 g
- Cholesterol 90 mg

Crispy Green Beans

Preparation Time: 10 minutes
Cooking Time: 8 minutes
Serve: 2

Ingredients:

- 1 egg, lightly beaten
- 1/2 lb green beans, stem removed
- ¼ tsp Italian seasoning
- 1 cup breadcrumbs
- Pepper
- Salt

Directions:

1. Preheat the air fryer to 400 F.
2. Spray air fryer basket with cooking spray.
3. Add egg to a shallow dish.
4. In a separate dish, mix breadcrumbs, Italian seasoning, pepper, and salt.
5. Dip green beans in egg then coat with breadcrumbs and place into the air fryer basket and cook for 8 minutes.
6. Serve and enjoy.

Nutritional Value (Amount per Serving):

- Calories 245
- Fat 7.1 g
- Carbohydrates 35.5 g
- Sugar 2.7 g
- Protein 10 g
- Cholesterol 89 mg

Flavors Baby Potatoes

Preparation Time: 10 minutes
Cooking Time: 20 minutes
Serve: 2

Ingredients:

- 12 oz baby potatoes
- 1/4 tsp ground cumin
- 1/4 tsp paprika
- 1/4 tsp chili powder
- 1/2 tbsp butter, melted
- 1/4 tsp pepper
- 1/2 tsp kosher salt

Directions:

1. Preheat the air fryer to 370 F.
2. Add all ingredients into the bowl and toss well.
3. Transfer potatoes into the air fryer basket and cook for 20 minutes. Stir halfway through.
4. Serve and enjoy.

Nutritional Value (Amount per Serving):

- Calories 135
- Fat 3.8 g
- Carbohydrates 22 g
- Sugar 0.2 g
- Protein 4.6 g
- Cholesterol 0 mg

Simple Carrot Fries

Preparation Time: 10 minutes
Cooking Time: 15 minutes
Serve: 2

Ingredients:

- 1/2 lb carrots, peeled and cut into fries shape
- 1/4 tsp ground cumin
- 1/2 tbsp olive oil
- 1/4 tsp paprika
- 1/2 tsp kosher salt

Directions:

1. Preheat the air fryer to 400 F.
2. In a large bowl, add all ingredients and toss until well coated.
3. Transfer carrot fries into the air fryer basket and cook for 15 minutes. Stir halfway through.
4. Serve and enjoy.

Nutritional Value (Amount per Serving):

- Calories 80
- Fat 3.6 g
- Carbohydrates 11.7 g
- Sugar 5.7 g
- Protein 1.1 g
- Cholesterol 0 mg

Herb Baby Potatoes

Preparation Time: 10 minutes
Cooking Time: 25 minutes
Serve: 2

Ingredients:

- 1 lb potatoes, cut into 1-inch pieces
- 1/4 tsp dried basil
- 1/4 tsp pepper
- 1/4 tsp dried oregano
- 1/4 tsp salt

Directions:

1. Preheat the air fryer to 400 F.
2. Add potatoes, basil, oregano, pepper, and salt in a bowl and toss well.
3. Transfer potatoes into the air fryer basket and cook for 25 minutes. Stir halfway through.
4. Serve and enjoy.

Nutritional Value (Amount per Serving):

- Calories 125
- Fat 0.2 g
- Carbohydrates 27.3 g
- Sugar 2.1 g
- Protein 3 g
- Cholesterol 0 mg

Nutritious Broccoli

Preparation Time: 10 minutes
Cooking Time: 20 minutes
Serve: 2

Ingredients:

- 1/2 lb broccoli florets
- 1 tbsp walnuts, chopped
- 1 tbsp olive oil
- 1 tbsp vinegar
- Pepper
- Salt

Directions:

1. Preheat the air fryer to 360 F.
2. Add all ingredients into the bowl and toss well. Add broccoli mixture into the air fryer basket and cook for 20 minutes. Stir halfway through.
3. Serve and enjoy.

Nutritional Value (Amount per Serving):

- Calories 130
- Fat 9.7 g
- Carbohydrates 8.9 g
- Sugar 2 g
- Protein 4.3 g
- Cholesterol 0 mg

Spicy Brussels Sprouts

Preparation Time: 10 minutes
Cooking Time: 14 minutes
Serve: 2

Ingredients:

- 1/2 lb Brussels sprouts, trimmed and halved
- 1/2 tsp cayenne
- 1/2 tbsp olive oil
- Pepper
- Salt

Directions:

1. Preheat the air fryer to 370 F.
2. Add all ingredients into the bowl and toss well.
3. Add Brussels sprouts mixture into the air fryer basket and cook for 14 minutes. Stir halfway through.
4. Serve and enjoy.

Nutritional Value (Amount per Serving):

- Calories 85
- Fat 4.1 g
- Carbohydrates 11 g
- Sugar 2.6 g
- Protein 4.1 g
- Cholesterol 0 mg

Lime Olive Potatoes

Preparation Time: 10 minutes
Cooking Time: 20 minutes
Serve: 2

Ingredients:

- 1 lb potatoes, peeled and cubed
- 1/2 cup olives, pitted and halved
- 1 tbsp olive oil
- 1/2 tbsp lime juice
- ¼ tsp chili powder
- 1/2 onion, sliced
- Pepper
- Salt

Directions:

1. Preheat the air fryer to 400 F.
2. Add all ingredients into the bowl and toss well.
3. Add potato olive mixture into the air fryer basket and cook for 20 minutes. Stir halfway through.
4. Serve and enjoy.

Nutritional Value (Amount per Serving):

- Calories 275
- Fat 11.1 g
- Carbohydrates 42.2 g
- Sugar 4.2 g
- Protein 4.7 g
- Cholesterol 0 mg

Tasty Baby Carrots

Preparation Time: 10 minutes
Cooking Time: 20 minutes
Serve: 2

Ingredients:

- 1/2 lb baby carrots, peeled
- ¼ tsp cinnamon
- 1 1/2 tbsp butter, melted
- Pepper
- Salt

Directions:

1. Preheat the air fryer to 380 F.
2. Add all ingredients into the bowl and toss well.
3. Add baby carrots into the air fryer basket and cook for 20 minutes. Stir halfway through.
4. Serve and enjoy.

Nutritional Value (Amount per Serving):

- Calories 120
- Fat 8.9 g
- Carbohydrates 10 g
- Sugar 5.4 g
- Protein 0.9 g
- Cholesterol 23 mg

Cherry Tomato & Green Beans

Preparation Time: 10 minutes
Cooking Time: 15 minutes
Serve: 2

Ingredients:

- 1/2 lb green beans, trimmed
- 1/4 cup parmesan cheese, shredded
- 1 tbsp butter, melted
- 1/2 cup cherry tomatoes, halved
- Pepper
- Salt

Directions:

1. Preheat the air fryer to 375 F.
2. In a bowl, toss green beans, cherry tomatoes, butter, pepper, and salt.
3. Add green beans and tomato mixture into the air fryer basket and cook for 15 minutes.
4. Sprinkle with cheese and serve.

Nutritional Value (Amount per Serving):

- Calories 142
- Fat 9.6 g
- Carbohydrates 10.3 g
- Sugar 2.8 g
- Protein 6.1 g
- Cholesterol 8 mg

Air Fried Zucchini & Squash

Preparation Time: 10 minutes
Cooking Time: 10 minutes
Serve: 2

Ingredients:

- 1 zucchini, sliced
- 1 tbsp butter, melted
- 1 yellow squash, sliced
- 2 tbsp parmesan cheese, grated
- 1 tsp garlic powder
- Pepper
- Salt

Directions:

1. Preheat the air fryer to 375 F.
2. Add all ingredients into the bowl and toss well.
3. Add vegetable mixture into the air fryer basket and cook for 10 minutes.
4. Serve and enjoy.

Nutritional Value (Amount per Serving):

- Calories 112
- Fat 8.4 g
- Carbohydrates 7.5 g
- Sugar 3.1 g
- Protein 4.2 g
- Cholesterol 4 mg

Chapter 5: Snack & Appetizers

Roasted Almonds

Preparation Time: 10 minutes
Cooking Time: 10 minutes
Serve: 8

Ingredients:

- 2 cups almonds
- ¼ tsp chili powder
- 1 tbsp butter, melted
- Salt

Directions:

1. Preheat the air fryer to 330 F.
2. Add almonds, chili powder, butter, and salt into the bowl and toss well.
3. Add almonds into the air fryer basket and cook for 10 minutes. Toss after every 3 minutes.
4. Serve and enjoy.

Nutritional Value (Amount per Serving):

- Calories 150
- Fat 13.3 g
- Carbohydrates 5.1 g
- Sugar 1 g
- Protein 5 g
- Cholesterol 4 mg

Crispy Onion Fritters

Preparation Time: 10 minutes
Cooking Time: 12 minutes
Serve: 4

Ingredients:

- 1 onion, sliced
- 2 tbsp olive oil
- ½ tbsp green chili paste
- ½ cup rice flour
- 1 cup chickpea flour
- ¼ tsp turmeric
- Pinch of baking soda
- Salt
- Water

Directions:

1. Add all ingredients except water into the bowl and mix until well combined. Slowly add water and mix until crumbly batter is formed.
2. Preheat the air fryer to 350 F.
3. Spray air fryer basket with cooking spray.
4. Make the medium size of fritters from the mixture and place into the air fryer basket and cook for 12 minutes. Flip fritters halfway through.
5. Serve and enjoy.

Nutritional Value (Amount per Serving):

- Calories 333
- Fat 10.5 g
- Carbohydrates 49.7 g
- Sugar 7.1 g
- Protein 11.3 g
- Cholesterol 1 mg

Spicy Chickpeas

Preparation Time: 10 minutes
Cooking Time: 30 minutes
Serve: 6

Ingredients:

- 30 oz can chickpeas, drained
- ½ tsp chili powder
- ¼ tsp cayenne
- 2 tbsp olive oil
- Salt

Directions:

1. Preheat the air fryer to 350 F.
2. In a bowl, toss chickpeas with oil and salt.
3. Add chickpeas into the air fryer basket and cook for 30 minutes. Shake basket halfway through.
4. Transfer chickpeas into the bowl. Add chili powder and cayenne and toss well.
5. Serve and enjoy.

Nutritional Value (Amount per Serving):

- Calories 235
- Fat 3.8 g
- Carbohydrates 40 g
- Sugar 6.2 g
- Protein 11.2 g
- Cholesterol 0 mg

Healthy Cashew Nuts

Preparation Time: 10 minutes
Cooking Time: 6 minutes
Serve: 2

Ingredients:

- 1 cup cashews
- 1 tsp ghee, melted
- ½ tsp chili powder
- Salt

Directions:

1. In a bowl, toss cashews with chili powder, ghee, and salt until well coated.
2. Add cashews into the air fryer basket and roast at 350 F for 5 minutes.
3. Toss cashews and roast for 1 minute more.

Nutritional Value (Amount per Serving):

- Calories 414
- Fat 34 g
- Carbohydrates 22.8 g
- Sugar 3.5 g
- Protein 10.6 g
- Cholesterol 5 mg

Nutritious Fox Nuts

Preparation Time: 10 minutes
Cooking Time: 10 minutes
Serve: 2

Ingredients:

- 1 1/2 cups fox nuts
- 1/8 tsp turmeric powder
- 1/4 tsp ground black pepper
- 1 tbsp ghee, melted
- Salt

Directions:

1. Preheat the air fryer to 350 F.
2. Add fox nuts, turmeric powder, pepper, salt, and melted ghee in a bowl and mix well.
3. Add fox nuts into the air fryer basket and cook for 10 minutes.
4. Serve and enjoy.

Nutritional Value (Amount per Serving):

- Calories 137
- Fat 6.9 g
- Carbohydrates 15.8 g
- Sugar 0 g
- Protein 3.8 g
- Cholesterol 16 mg

Potato Patties

Preparation Time: 10 minutes
Cooking Time: 12 minutes
Serve: 5

Ingredients:

- 2 potatoes, cooked, peel & mashed
- 2 tbsp cornflour
- ½ tsp ground cumin
- ¼ tsp turmeric
- 1 tbsp ginger garlic paste
- 1 small onion, chopped
- 1 tsp green chili paste
- Salt

Directions:

1. Add all ingredients into the bowl and mix until well combined.
2. Preheat the air fryer to 350 F.
3. Spray air fryer basket with cooking spray.
4. Make equal shapes of patties from the mixture and place them into the air fryer basket and cook for 12 minutes. Turn patties halfway through.
5. Serve and enjoy.

Nutritional Value (Amount per Serving):

- Calories 80
- Fat 0.4 g
- Carbohydrates 17.5 g
- Sugar 1.9 g
- Protein 1.9 g
- Cholesterol 0 mg

Broccoli Bites

Preparation Time: 10 minutes
Cooking Time: 15 minutes
Serve: 4

Ingredients:

- 2 cups cottage cheese, grated
- 1 cup broccoli, minced
- ½ tsp turmeric
- ¼ cup chickpea flour
- ½ tsp chili powder
- 1 tbsp ginger garlic paste
- Salt

Directions:

1. Add grated cottage cheese, broccoli, and remaining ingredients into the bowl and mix until well combined.
2. Preheat the air fryer to 400 F.
3. Spray air fryer basket with cooking spray.
4. Make small balls from cottage cheese mixture and place them into the air fryer basket and cook for 15 minutes. Turn balls halfway through.
5. Serve and enjoy.

Nutritional Value (Amount per Serving):

- Calories 137
- Fat 2.1 g
- Carbohydrates 12.5 g
- Sugar 4.8 g
- Protein 17.1 g
- Cholesterol 5 mg

Corn on the Cob

Preparation Time: 10 minutes
Cooking Time: 20 minutes
Serve: 4

Ingredients:

- 4 ears of corn, husked
- 1 tbsp butter, melted
- ½ lemon juice
- Salt

Directions:

1. Brush corn with melted butter and season with salt.
2. Preheat the air fryer to 400 F.
3. Place corn into the air fryer basket and cook for 15-20 minutes.
4. Drizzle lemon juice over corn and serve.

Nutritional Value (Amount per Serving):

- Calories 157
- Fat 4.7 g
- Carbohydrates 29 g
- Sugar 5 g
- Protein 5 g
- Cholesterol 8 mg

Crispy Okra

Preparation Time: 10 minutes
Cooking Time: 12 minutes
Serve: 4

Ingredients:

- 10 oz okra, wash & pat dry
- ¼ cup semolina
- ½ cup rice flour
- 1 cup water
- ¾ tsp chili powder
- ½ tsp turmeric
- ½ tsp ground cumin
- Salt

Directions:

1. Slice okra lengthwise in quarters.
2. In a bowl, add rice flour, ground cumin, semolina, turmeric, chili powder, and salt and mix well.
3. Slowly pour water into the rice flour mixture and mix until a thick batter is formed.
4. Add okra into the batter and mix until well coated and set aside for 10 minutes.
5. Spray air fryer basket with cooking spray.
6. Preheat the air fryer to 330 F.
7. Place okra into the air fryer basket and cook for 10 minutes.
8. Remove air fryer basket and shake the okra and cook at 350 F for 2 minutes more.
9. Serve and enjoy.

Nutritional Value (Amount per Serving):

- Calories 143
- Fat 0.7 g
- Carbohydrates 29.4 g
- Sugar 1.1 g
- Protein 4 g
- Cholesterol 0 mg

Easy Banana Chips

Preparation Time: 10 minutes
Cooking Time: 15 minutes
Serve: 2

Ingredients:

- 1 large raw bananas, peel and sliced
- 1/4 tsp turmeric powder
- 1 tsp olive oil
- 1 tsp salt

Directions:

1. In a bowl add water, turmeric powder, and salt. Stir well.
2. Add sliced bananas in bowl water soak for 10 minutes. Drain well and pat dry chips with a paper towel.
3. Add banana slices to a bowl and toss with oil and salt.
4. Place banana slices into the air fryer basket and cook at 350 F for 15 minutes. Turn halfway through.
5. Serve and enjoy.

Nutritional Value (Amount per Serving):

- Calories 84
- Fat 2.7 g
- Carbohydrates 16.1 g
- Sugar 8.4 g
- Protein 0.8 g
- Cholesterol 0 mg

Sweet Potato Bites

Preparation Time: 10 minutes
Cooking Time: 15 minutes
Serve: 2

Ingredients:

- 2 sweet potato, diced into 1-inch cubes
- 2 tbsp olive oil
- 2 tbsp honey
- 1 1/2 tsp cinnamon

Directions:

1. Preheat the air fryer to 350 F.
2. Add all ingredients into the bowl and toss well.
3. Add sweet potato into the air fryer basket and cook for 15 minutes.
4. Serve and enjoy.

Nutritional Value (Amount per Serving):

- Calories 301
- Fat 14.3 g
- Carbohydrates 43.2 g
- Sugar 24.8 g
- Protein 2.9 g
- Cholesterol 0 mg

Fish Nuggets

Preparation Time: 10 minutes
Cooking Time: 10 minutes
Serve: 4

Ingredients:

- 3 eggs, lightly beaten
- 1 lb cod fish fillet, cut into chunks
- 1/4 cup olive oil
- 1 cup all-purpose flour
- 1 tsp garlic powder
- 1 cup breadcrumbs
- 1/4 tsp pepper
- 1 tsp salt

Directions:

1. Preheat the air fryer to 400 F.
2. In a small bowl, add eggs and whisk well.
3. In a separate bowl, add flour.
4. In a shallow dish, mix together breadcrumbs, garlic powder, pepper, salt, and oil.
5. Dip fish chunks into the egg then roll in flour and coat with breadcrumb mixture.
6. Place coated nuggets into the air fryer basket and cook at 400 F for 10 minutes.
7. Serve and enjoy.

Nutritional Value (Amount per Serving):

- Calories 497
- Fat 18.6 g
- Carbohydrates 44.1 g
- Sugar 2.2 g
- Protein 37 g
- Cholesterol 185 mg

Flavorful Chickpeas

Preparation Time: 10 minutes
Cooking Time: 10 minutes
Serve: 4

Ingredients:

- 14 oz can chickpeas, drained and rinsed
- 1 tbsp Parmesan cheese, grated
- 1/8 tsp garlic powder
- 1 tbsp olive oil
- 1/8 tsp cayenne
- Pepper
- Salt

Directions:

1. Preheat the air fryer to 400 F.
2. Add all ingredients into the bowl and toss well.
3. Add chickpeas into the air fryer basket and cook for 10 minutes. Stir halfway through.
4. Serve and enjoy.

Nutritional Value (Amount per Serving):

- Calories 155
- Fat 5.3 g
- Carbohydrates 22.8 g
- Sugar 0 g
- Protein 5.8 g
- Cholesterol 2 mg

Sweet Potato Fries

Preparation Time: 10 minutes
Cooking Time: 20 minutes
Serve: 2

Ingredients:

- 1 sweet potato, peeled and cut into fries shape
- 2 tsp olive oil
- 1/8 tsp cayenne
- 1/4 tsp chili powder
- Pepper
- Salt

Directions:

1. Preheat the air fryer to 400 F.
2. Spray air fryer basket with cooking spray.
3. Add all ingredients into the bowl and toss well.
4. Add sweet potato fries into the air fryer basket and cook for 20 minutes. Turn halfway through.
5. Serve and enjoy.

Nutritional Value (Amount per Serving):

- Calories 95
- Fat 4.8 g
- Carbohydrates 12 g
- Sugar 3.7 g
- Protein 1.2 g
- Cholesterol 0 mg

Healthy Pumpkin Seeds

Preparation Time: 10 minutes

Cooking Time: 10 minutes

Serve: 8

Ingredients:

- 2 cups pumpkin seeds
- 2 tbsp brown sugar
- 1 tsp vinegar
- 1 tbsp olive oil
- 1 tsp kosher salt

Directions:

1. Preheat the air fryer to 325 F.
2. Add all ingredients into the bowl and toss well.
3. Add pumpkin seeds into the air fryer basket and cook for 10 minutes. Stir halfway through.
4. Serve and enjoy.

Nutritional Value (Amount per Serving):

- Calories 210
- Fat 17.6 g
- Carbohydrates 8.4 g
- Sugar 2.6 g
- Protein 8.5 g
- Cholesterol 0 mg

Chapter 6: 30-Day Meal Plan

Day 1

Breakfast-Healthy Egg Bites

Lunch- Healthy Salmon Patties

Dinner-Parmesan White Fish Fillets

Day 2

Breakfast-Easy Potato wedges

Lunch- Quick & Easy Salmon Patties

Dinner-Bagel Crust White Fish Fillets

Day 3

Breakfast-Sweet Potatoes & Brussels sprouts

Lunch- Flavors Crab Cakes

Dinner-Pesto White Fish Fillets

Day 4

Breakfast-Healthy Spinach Frittata

Lunch- Creamy Scallops

Dinner-Everything Bagel Salmon

Day 5

Breakfast-Breakfast Potatoes

Lunch- Cajun Scallops

Dinner-Tasty Pesto Salmon

Day 6

Breakfast-Spinach Pepper Egg Bites

Lunch- Quick & Easy Scallops

Dinner-Cheesy Salmon

Day 7

Breakfast-Egg Cheese Muffins

Lunch- Easy Salmon Patties

Dinner-Flavorful Salmon Steak

Day 8

Breakfast-Mushroom Spinach Muffins

Lunch- Tasty Tuna Cakes

Dinner-Healthy Cod Fish Fillets

Day 9

Breakfast-Egg Veggie Soufflé

Lunch- Scallops with Sauce

Dinner-Shrimp with Veggie

Day 10

Breakfast-Italian Egg Muffins

Lunch- Flavorful Spicy Shrimp

Dinner-Shrimp Dinner

Day 11

Breakfast-Healthy Egg Bites

Lunch- Tasty Shrimp Fajitas

Dinner-Shrimp Boil

Day 12

Breakfast-Easy Potato wedges

Lunch- Flavorful Tuna Patties

Dinner-BBQ Salmon

Day 13

Breakfast-Sweet Potatoes & Brussels sprouts

Lunch- Cheesy Tuna Patties

Dinner-Tasty Tuna Steaks

Day 14

Breakfast-Healthy Spinach Frittata

Lunch- Delicious Tuna Patties

Dinner-Easy Lemon Dill Fish Fillets

Day 15

Breakfast-Breakfast Potatoes

Lunch- Crispy Catfish Fillets

Dinner-Pesto Mahi Mahi

Day 16

Breakfast-Healthy Egg Bites

Lunch- Healthy Salmon Patties

Dinner-Parmesan White Fish Fillets

Day 17

Breakfast-Easy Potato wedges

Lunch- Quick & Easy Salmon Patties

Dinner-Bagel Crust White Fish Fillets

Day 18

Breakfast-Sweet Potatoes & Brussels sprouts

Lunch- Flavors Crab Cakes

Dinner-Pesto White Fish Fillets

Day 19

Breakfast-Healthy Spinach Frittata

Lunch- Creamy Scallops

Dinner-Everything Bagel Salmon

Day 20

Breakfast-Breakfast Potatoes

Lunch- Cajun Scallops

Dinner-Tasty Pesto Salmon

Day 21

Breakfast-Spinach Pepper Egg Bites

Lunch- Quick & Easy Scallops

Dinner-Cheesy Salmon

Day 22

Breakfast-Egg Cheese Muffins

Lunch- Easy Salmon Patties

Dinner-Flavorful Salmon Steak

Day 23

Breakfast-Mushroom Spinach Muffins

Lunch- Tasty Tuna Cakes

Dinner-Healthy Cod Fish Fillets

Day 24

Breakfast-Egg Veggie Soufflé

Lunch- Scallops with Sauce

Dinner-Shrimp with Veggie

Day 25

Breakfast-Italian Egg Muffins

Lunch- Flavorful Spicy Shrimp

Dinner-Shrimp Dinner

Day 26

Breakfast-Healthy Egg Bites

Lunch- Tasty Shrimp Fajitas

Dinner-Shrimp Boil

Day 27

Breakfast-Easy Potato wedges

Lunch- Flavorful Tuna Patties

Dinner-BBQ Salmon

Day 28

Breakfast-Sweet Potatoes & Brussels sprouts

Lunch- Cheesy Tuna Patties

Dinner-Tasty Tuna Steaks

Day 29

Breakfast-Healthy Spinach Frittata

Lunch- Delicious Tuna Patties

Dinner-Easy Lemon Dill Fish Fillets

Day 30

Breakfast-Breakfast Potatoes

Lunch- Crispy Catfish Fillets

Dinner-Pesto Mahi Mahi

Conclusion

The Pescatarian diet is one of the similar diet plans compare with the Mediterranean diet because both the diet is focused on vegetarian food and allows seafood to meet their protein requirements. The Pescatarian diet completely avoids meats, poultry, pork, and lamb because they contain saturated fat. Some of the Pescatarian diet followers allow eggs and dairy products into their products but some are not as it is their personal preference. The Pescatarian word is made an Italic world 'peace means 'fish, and vegetarian. Fish and seafood like crab, oyster, shrimp, and more are some of the primary sources of protein in the Pescatarian diet.

This cookbook contains tasty, healthy and delicious Pescatarian diet recipes that come from different categories like breakfast, fish, seafood, vegetable, side dishes, snacks, appetizers. The recipes written in this book are unique and written into an easily understandable form. All the recipes are written with their preparation and cooking time followed by step-by-step cooking instructions. The recipes written in this book are ends with their nutritional value information. The nutritional value information will help to keep track of daily calorie consumption.

9 781954 703179